TENDING YOUR MONEY GARDEN™

May your money garden flourish.

Bob Dreizler

12/2/98

by Bob Dreizler
Chartered Financial Consultant

Illustrated by Bob Armstrong

Published by
Rossonya Books

Designed by Jenni Haas Design

Library of Congress #98-091581
Publisher's Cataloging-in-Publication
(Provided by Quality Books, Inc.)
Dreizler, Bob.
Tending your money garden / by Bob Dreizler; illustrated by Bob Armstrong.
p. cm.
Includes bibliographical references.
ISBN: 0-9663139-0-9
1. Finance, Personal. I. Armstrong, Bob (Robert E.) 1950- II. Title.

HG179.D74 1998   332.04
                              QBI98-818

TENDING YOUR MONEY GARDEN BOOK™
CONTENTS

Dedicated to my mom and dad.
Thanks

Acknowledgments

When I decided to write Tending Your Money Garden, two dreams motivated me. I wanted to write a good book, and I wanted to hold that book in my hands on my fiftieth birthday. I could not have done either without the help and encouragement of family, friends and advisors.

Throughout the process, my assistant's assistance was invaluable. Debbie Costello kept my financial consulting and tax business operating smoothly while I wrote and rewrote. The encouragement and technical support she provided were invaluable.

Jenni Haas has helped display my words and ideas in a captivating format ever since my media guru, the gentle Laurie McCann, suggested I start writing my newsletter four yeas ago. With Jenni's help, I knew I could create a great looking book.

Jenni introduced me to the artistic renderings of Bob Armstrong, the illustrator of this book. He had the ability to transform my visions into scenes filled with happy characters.

Author Charlotte Higgins became my book coach six months before this book went to the printer. Our weekly talks helped me stay focused, positive and calm.

Freelance writer Lynn Narlesky had the burdensome job of reading my several drafts and offering crucial advice that helped make this book more readable (such as convincing me to use fewer parentheses). Angie Williamson and Sonya Dreizler also provided crucial editing assistance.

George Gay, Jack Brill and my friends with First Affirmative Financial Network deserve special appreciation for being who they are and doing what they do. I've never known so many great people to work for one organization.

The wonderful people at Rossonya Books were always there for us. They worked as hard to self-publish this book as Debbie and I did.

Thanks to my teenage children, Ross and Sonya, for constantly being sources of material and inspiration for my writing. Assuming they noticed my absences from home, I hope they didn't mind.

Finally, I want to thank my wonderful wife Stacey for her tolerance of my obsessive behavior, for her editing skills, and for allowing me to share some of the high and low moments from our financial life.

WELCOME TO YOUR MONEY GARDEN

Money is a singular thing. It ranks with love as man's
greatest source of joy. And with death as
his greatest source of anxiety.

John Kenneth Galbraith, economist, The Age of Uncertainty

Welcome to Your Money Garden

The gratification of wealth is not found in the mere possession or in lavish expenditure, but in its wise application.
Miguel de Cervantes

Welcome to Tending Your Money Garden, a how-to primer about enhancing your money-growing skills. More importantly, this book will help you cultivate your dreams.

For over twenty years I've worked with individuals, couples, and families to facilitate their financial evolution. As a result, it no longer surprises me when smart and successful people shyly confess that they don't understand certain basic financial concepts. So I wrote a book specifically for people who thought they'd never buy a money management book.

Good financial advice is cheap and easy to find. Monetary success, however, requires two things: a sincere commitment to your goals, and the discipline to consistently implement some simple concepts.

Tending Your Money Garden is not a comprehensive text on financial planning. It won't offer hot stock tips or outline cold-hearted investment strategies. Instead, it will offer a simple mixture of practical advice, humor, and helpful analogies.

If you prefer complex and boring personal finance books, please refer to my four volume trilogy, *The Quantitative Explication of Pecuniary Maximization Techniques* (soon to become a made-for-TV movie retitled "The Alien Abduction of Fluorine, the Naughty Dental Hygienist").

This book may not cause you to start reading *The Wall Street Journal* in your herb garden, but I hope it will provide you with three things:
- an increased commitment to making your dreams come true,
- a greater awareness of your financial situation, and
- some practical money management skills.

Because many people care as much about where their money grows as how rapidly it grows, I'm including a section on "values-based investing." More commonly referred to as "socially responsible investing," this is my professional specialty.

I've tried to avoid using financial jargon, but if you don't understand a word or phrase, please check the glossary. Maybe that term will be there and maybe it won't; glossaries are like that.

Illustrations, charts, and graphs should help you to visualize important concepts. The Workbook Section includes sample forms to help you implement your goals, and the Resources Chapter lists some books and websites so you can learn more.

Exploring Your Money Garden

Managing money is like tending a garden. This long-term process takes foresight, patience, and commitment. It also takes planning and goal-setting. When gardening, you quickly learn that if you don't start planting your seeds until your neighbors are harvesting their crops, you won't have much to show for your efforts.

The steps along the paths to both blooming blossoms and flourishing finances are quite similar. Both start with visions. Once you design a plan, you begin to till the soil using the appropriate tools. Planting the seeds is followed by a continuous process of watering and nourishing your plants. All the while, you must protect your crops from predators, diseases and unpredictable weather.

If you are diligent and suffer few misfortunes, a bountiful harvest will result. Ultimately, you consume your crops or consummate your dreams.

Some people can tend their financial garden by themselves; others benefit from using outside advisors such as financial planners, estate attorneys, and vegetarian insurance agents. This book may allow you to do much of the work yourself. It should also help you identify times when professional assistance is needed.

I'm a sucker for analogies and metaphors, so I'm warning you that I'll be using them throughout this book. The garden analogy, however, will be used in moderation. This decision saves you from reading the tenuous analogy that would have been on page 34 when I compared selling stock options short with semi-circular raking techniques.

I hope this book will become a valuable tool for tending *your* money garden.

PLANTING THE SEEDS

EVERY SPRING GARDENERS PLANT TINY SEEDS IN THEIR SOIL. MUCH LATER, THESE BLOOM INTO LARGE PLANTS. THE PROCESS OF GROWING MONEY IS SIMILAR. SMALL AMOUNTS OF MONEY COMBINED WITH CONTINUOUS EFFORT CAN PRODUCE THE ABUNDANCE THAT WILL ALLOW YOU TO HAVE MORE OPTIONS AND TO FULFILL YOUR DREAMS.

DREAMS ARE THE SEEDLINGS OF REALITIES.
JAMES ALLEN

IT's ONLY MONEY,
BUT MONEY BUYS YOU OPTIONS

IT'S PRETTY HARD TO TELL WHAT BRINGS HAPPINESS;
POVERTY AND WEALTH HAVE BOTH FAILED.
KIN HUBBARD

Money is more than just a commodity to accumulate; it is a resource that provides you with options. In theory, more options mean more freedom.

Despite how you may feel about money's impact on you and society, all people need some to survive. Good thoughts and kind deeds alone buy neither bread nor a month-long vacation in South America.

Being rich does not necessarily make you happy, but neither does being poor. Those with more money and more options aren't necessarily happier than those with less. Numerous academic studies have proven this. Unfortunately, their accuracy is questioned because the surveys were financed by happy rich people.

Each of us could live a more humble existence by learning to survive on less. Remember what it was like just after you moved away from home for the third time? Most of us survived and acquired lots of character, but it would have been nice to have had a few more financial options.

Riding the Financial Roller Coaster

After my wife and I graduated from college, we had what seemed like a surplus of cash. We make a lot more today, but sometimes it seems we don't have enough for our current financial goals.

In the early 1970s we had few commitments. We were too young to worry about retirement and didn't have kids yet, so we twice squirreled away money, quit our jobs, and traveled for four months. Life seemed easy.

A few years after our trip to Europe, we sat in our '67 Ford Maverick outside a finance company office preparing to sign forms to get a $1000 loan. My pregnant wife sat in the front seat next to me, crying. We felt trapped; we had few options. Getting that loan seemed like the only option available to pay our bills.

Our short-term goal at that moment was a rather humble one: we just wanted to temporarily ease our financial stress. Over time, our financial situation improved and options expanded. Though our financial stress level decreased, it never disappeared. The challenges never leave, they just evolve.

Life is a constant financial roller coaster ride. We have all struggled with dilemmas caused by the lack of money, but sometimes receiving an unexpected influx of money can be a dilemma in itself. When your situation is beyond your control, learn to hang on tight and try to manage your emotions.

Most of the time you can take control of your life by managing your money better. Prudent financial planning won't necessarily make your life happier, but it should reduce your stress and allow you to expand your options.

Turning Your Dreams into Reality

Without dreams, your money becomes purely a survival tool, a means of measuring your wealth against that of your neighbors or parents. Well-defined dreams will motivate you, but you need direction to arrive at your intended destination. You must be committed to accumulating money to attain

personal financial goals such as:
- buying a new house or vacation home,
- retiring from work early,
- helping fund your child's education,
- taking a fantasy vacation,
- supporting an important charitable or political cause,
- starting your own business, or even
- writing a book.

An exciting part of living in the moment can be planning for the future—directing your life toward a certain path that will make your future more fulfilling than your present. No one likes making sacrifices, but having well-defined dreams helps make your immediate sacrifices less burdensome.

So, whether your most vivid dream is to double the size of your garden or take a trip around the world, working toward that goal means developing a plan and investing regularly.

What are your dreams?

Are you really committed to fulfilling some specific goals or to realizing your dreams? The Workbook Section of this book includes a page where you can commit these to paper: your short-term, intermediate-term and long-term goals and dreams.

ALL THAT WE SEE OR SEEM
IS BUT A DREAM WITHIN A
DREAM.

EDGAR ALLAN POE, "A
DREAM WITHIN A DREAM"

LACK OF MONEY

IF I NEVER HAD A CENT, I'D BE RICH AS ROCKERFELLER.
FRANK SINATRA, "ON THE SUNNY SIDE OF THE STREET"
(J. McHUGH- D. FIELDS)

What is the greatest obstacle is between you and your dreams? Most people would answer—lack of money. That's hard to argue with, though some incredibly rich people can never fulfill their dreams, and those of more modest means are content to pursue attainable dreams while living a happy life.

There are two basic ways to have more money: 1) earn more, or 2) manage your money more efficiently. To make more you have two choices: 1) work more hours, or 2) find a creative way to generate additional income. To explore this last option, check out junk e-mails or buy a get-rich-quick book. Who knows, maybe you *can* earn an additional $10,000 a week milking venom from cobras in the comfort of your home, or by starting a multi-level marketing operation that starts multi-level marketing operations, but good money management may be easier.

There is a lot of truth to the saying "You have to have money to make money," but money is a relative commodity. Accept what you can do, live within your means, develop realistic goals, then start investing.

I'm often asked, "Do I have enough money to start investing?" Sometimes this question is asked by individuals with less than a hundred dollars in the bank, but occasionally an individual thinks $20,000 isn't enough.

It is important that you first accumulate an *emergency fund*—enough in your savings to provide for the uncertainties of your *cash flow*. Three months of income is a common guideline for this figure, but if you have adequate insurance and can accept the risks involved, a much smaller amount may be sufficient. There are no magic formulas; you'll need to learn what works best for you.

Don't delay the *process* of starting to invest just because you haven't saved much so far. Develop an investment mentality. Read the business section of your local newspaper. Subscribe to a financial magazine. Even emptying your piggy bank may yield enough to make a down-payment on your dream—*provided this amount buys your commitment to improve your financial habits.*

MONEY IS COINED LIBERTY.
DOSTOEVSKY

GROWING YOUR AWARENESS

LONG-RANGE PLANNING DOES NOT DEAL WITH FUTURE DECISIONS,
BUT WITH THE FUTURE OF PRESENT DECISIONS.
PETER DRUCKER

Many people get into financial difficulty and fail to achieve their dreams. This is not because of things they knowingly did wrong, but because they didn't or wouldn't acquire an awareness of the specifics of their current financial situation.

Getting overwhelmed with credit card debt is the most apparent manifestation of this problem. Saving too little for that dream vacation is less obvious. The following techniques can help you:
- focus on your day-to-day spending habits,
- acquire an awareness of your progress in reducing your debts and accumulating assets, and
- quantify the progress you are making toward achieving your dreams.

The one month budget

When people think about acquiring more of an awareness of their financial situation, the first thing that comes to mind is budgeting. The dreaded "B" word is one of the most disturbing words in the English language. Having a budget implies keeping track of where each penny goes and feeling guilty in the process.

Most attempts to budget fail because the budget scheme is prepared with little factual data. Despite how well you estimate your spending money, five to twenty percent is "mystery money" that just disappears.

I suggest that you keep track of every dollar for just one month. By the end of the month you will know where your mystery money is going. This alone should reduce frivolous spending.

HAVE MORE THAN THOU SHOWEST, SPEAK LESS THAN THOU KNOWEST.

WILLIAM SHAKESPEARE

It can be very disturbing to discover how much you actually spend on some of your minor extravagances and vices: fast food, alcohol, lottery tickets, cigarettes, peach-scented body ointments, etc. You'll find that small, but regular expenditures do add up. If you spend $1.50 a day on coffee, that means you are spending over $500 per year to keep caffeine flowing through your veins.

During the next month, keep track of all your purchases. A computer program like Quicken® can help. These expenditures can then be sorted by category so you can really see how much you spend. Once you've gathered the data, you can decide what changes you need to make.

Chart Your Money

Keep a money chart? Most people think this idea is a crazy one. My wife did initially, but I believe that anything is worth trying if it helps motivate you to accumulate assets or pay off debts.

The chart in this chapter is a shrunken copy of the chart I kept while my wife and I were in our late twenties and early thirties. In 1975, we had just returned from a four-month, 15,000 mile trip. We traveled around the U.S. and Canada without our car, living quite frugally. Fru-

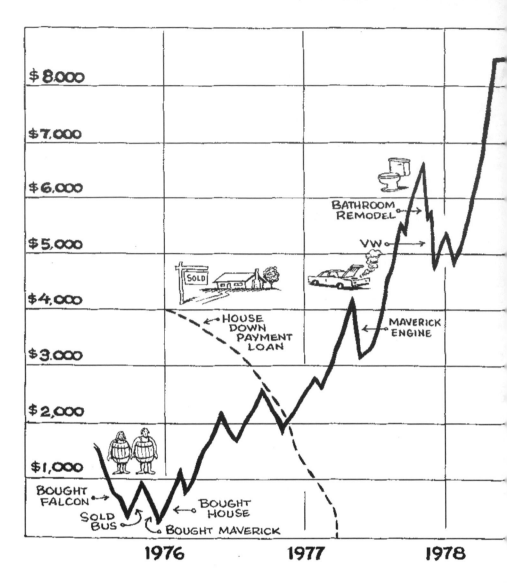

$8,000
$7,000
$6,000
$5,000
$4,000
$3,000
$2,000
$1,000

BATHROOM REMODEL
VW
HOUSE DOWN PAYMENT LOAN
MAVERICK ENGINE

BOUGHT FALCON
SOLD BUS
BOUGHT HOUSE
BOUGHT MAVERICK

1976   1977   1978

gal may be an understatement.

After returning to Sacramento, we started planning our next big adventure—an extended trip to Europe. One of the immediate drawbacks was our lack of money. We had $1000 and were living in our VW bus parked in front of Mary Lynn and Lee's house.

One day, on my way to substitute teaching, the engine of the van died. Anyone who has ever owned an old VW bus can relate to this. So we sold our dead bus, bought a beat-up Ford Falcon for $200, and moved into a less than luxurious apartment. So much for our savings.

By the beginning of 1976, our assets totaled $200. See low point on

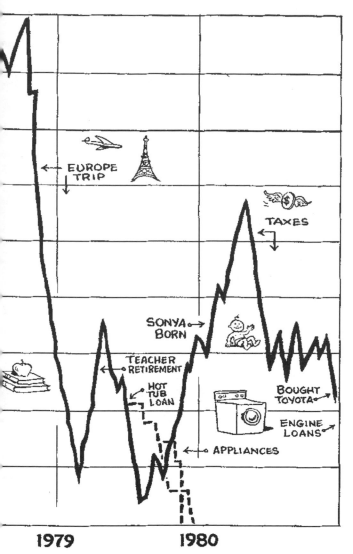

EUROPE
TRIP

TAXES

SONYA
BORN

TEACHER
RETIREMENT

HOT
TUB
LOAN

BOUGHT
TOYOTA

ENGINE
LOANS

APPLIANCES

1979   1980

chart. I know this sounds like a TV infomercial, but a month later we bought our first house, thanks to loans of $3600 from our skeptical, but loving parents.

We weren't sure if we could handle the monthly mortgage payment of $270, but we did and more. Motivated by the vision of our European adventure, we saved diligently and paid off the loans to our parents within eighteen months. An obsession with getting rid of the dotted line on the chart helped motivate us.

We built our assets up to $8,000 over the next two-and-a-half years, then quit our jobs again and took off for a memorable season in Europe.

Once we returned, our money chart again fluctuated up and down based on various purchases, windfalls and the birth of our daughter, Sonya.

About 1981, I stopped doing the chart. It became too unwieldy—about three feet high and four feet long. It started on one closet wall, turned the corner, and took over another wall.

The figures on my chart came from keeping track of how much money we had in various places—savings and checking accounts, investments, and even what was in our wallets. Stacey somehow tolerated this, as well as my weekly accounting of where all our money was spent. While you may not wish to decorate your walls with blue-squared graph paper, this technique may facilitate communication with your partner on money issues. NOTE: I do not recommend the chart unless you have a stable relationship or marriage.

I'm not so visibly obsessive anymore. I can find out what we owe and own quickly, but I only total our assets and liabilities once a year now.

Depending on your situation and temperament, money charting may help you visualize your financial progress. Whether you use the latest software or old-fashioned ledger paper, this technique clearly cultivates good money habits and documents your success.

Year End Balance Sheet

New Year's Day offers a wonderful opportunity to make financial commitments. This may not be your top priority though if you had one too many organically fermented grape-based beverages the night before.

However, this activity might sound appealing if the only alternative is watching The Starbuck's™ Coffee Latte Bowl and its dramatic pigskin showdown between the Durango State Deranged Dobermen and the Fightin' Flautists of the Missoula Institute of Music.

One of the best ways to acquire an awareness of your current financial situation is by listing the value of your assets: house, retirement plans, savings accounts and investments. Then list your liabilities or debts. Divide your debts into:
- long-term liabilities such as home mortgage,
- your medium-term debts including car loans and lines of credit, and
- your short-term credit card-type debts.

If your total assets exceed your liabilities, this is your net worth. If your liabilities exceed your assets, let's just say you are "asset-challenged."

The true value of your new-found awareness

THERE WAS A TIME WHEN A FOOL AND HIS MONEY WERE SOON PARTED, BUT NOW IT HAPPENS TO EVERYBODY.
ADLAI STEVENSON

won't come until next year when you will see how your assets have grown and how your debts have withered.

January is an ideal time to do this since tax and investment statements arrive with actual figures for many of these amounts. If you aren't reading this book in December or January, do this exercise soon so you can see how rapidly you can increase your net worth between now and next year.

BALANCE SHEET

ASSETS		LIABILITIES	
		Long-Term Debts	
Personal Residence	$250,000	First Mortgage	$178,000
		Second Mortgage	$22,000
Rental Property	$155,000	Mortgage (Rental)	
$102,000			
Personal Property	$20,000		
Automobile	$12,000	Auto Loans	$3,000
Investment Assets		**Medium Term Debt**	
Mutual Funds	$25,000		
Stocks	$15,000	Personal Loans	$5,000
Retirement Plans	$100,000		
Certificates of Deposit	$10,000	**Short Term Debt**	
Savings Accounts	$3,000	Credit Cards	$1,000
Checking Account	$1,000		
TOTAL ASSETS	**$591,000**	**LIABILITIES**	**$311,000**

NET WORTH = $280,000

Balancing your checkbook

I'm constantly amazed when some of my competent, street-wise clients tell me that they have never balanced their checkbook. Rather than tackle this perplexing task, they keep hundreds to thousands of extra dollars in a non-interest bearing account to compensate for the ambiguity of their balance.

With available computer programs, this can be a less daunting task than it used to be. As with any new duty, this monthly bonding-with-your-money experience will take time to master. However, once you become competent at this, you will feel more comfortable while managing other areas of your finances.

OBSTACLES CANNOT CRUSH ME.
EVERY OBSTACLE YIELDS TO
STERN RESOLVE. HE WHO IS
FIXED TO A STAR DOES NOT
CHANGE HIS MIND.

LEONARDO DA VINCI C.1500

BATTLE OF THE SELVES

HE DOES NOT POSSESS WEALTH THAT ALLOWS IT TO POSSESS HIM.
BENJAMIN FRANKLIN

Some of the hardest financial decisions you will ever make involve whether to live a higher lifestyle today or sacrifice and save for tomorrow. Sometimes neither option is available because you first have to pay off bills from your past indulgences. This dilemma is what I mean by Battle of the Selves.

Few people have excess money. If they do, it's only for a short time —until they figure out how to pump up their lifestyle and find ways to spend their surplus. Whether you go out Friday night with $20 or $50 in your pocket, you'll likely come home with none. The same is true with larger amounts of money.

Most money is spent by your Current Self. (CS) That's the only Self who carries a wallet and has immediate survival needs such as eating, finding shelter and watching prerecorded celebrity sporting events on cable TV. Your CS realizes you *must* squirrel away some money for your Future Self (FS) in order to do special things like buy houses, take legendary vacations and retire in comfort.

Even though your Current Self realizes all of this, it takes a mature CS to actually deny immediate pleasure so FS can have some of that pleasure later—if there's any money left over. If your Past Self (PS) was not very responsible, as PSs tend to be, CS's lifestyle suffers. Until PS's bills are paid off, your FS receives nothing.

Throughout life you are constantly deciding how to allocate your limited funds among these three Selves. This situation is even more complicated if you also have to deal with the Current Selves, Past Selves and Future Selves of your spouse, ex-spouses, and children.

Be aware of this perpetual conflict, and remember: once you pay off your Past Self, you only have to divide your money between two of you.

TOOLS AND STRATEGIES

IN ORDER TO NURTURE YOUR CROPS, YOU NEED TO POSSESS THE
RIGHT TOOLS AND USE THEM PROPERLY. YOU ALSO NEED TO USE
STRATEGIES TO ENHANCE THE GROWTH OF YOUR CROPS.
IN MONEY MANAGEMENT, TOOLS CAN BE THE INVESTMENTS
YOU PUT YOUR MONEY INTO, OR THEY CAN BE THE RESOURCES
YOU USE TO ENHANCE THIS PROCESS. STRATEGIES CAN BE AS SIMPLE
AS DISCIPLINE AND PATIENCE OR AS COMPLEX AS INVESTMENT POLICIES.

12

TWELVE PRUDENT MONEY MANAGEMENT RULES

1. Spend less money and consume more efficiently.

2. Pay yourself just like you would pay a utility company. **Make** yourself put a specific dollar amount or percentage of your monthly income into a special savings account or mutual fund. Use more than one account if you have other future needs, such as saving for a child's education or buying a home.

3. Avoid the use of credit cards if possible (especially ones with 18% or higher interest rates). Use consumer loans only to finance major items that are **essential**. Save up, then buy other items later with cash. Keep one credit card for emergencies, identification and short-term needs. Destroy and cancel the rest. Pay off balances as rapidly as possible.

4. Give yourself a specific amount of cash each month that you are allowed to spend on non-essential or frivolous items.

5. If you don't already own a house, begin saving to buy one. This is one of the best investments and tax breaks available.

6. Begin building a retirement fund **now**. Maximize contributions to tax-deductible and employer-subsidized retirement plans. Defer taxes by using mutual funds, stocks, annuities and perhaps life insurance. To enjoy a comfortable, early retirement, hide money from yourself in as many places as possible.

7. Acquire a basic knowledge of taxes. Know what is deductible and keep good records.

8. Each January set specific, realistic financial goals you would like to meet during the coming year. For example: "Put $2,000 into an investment program," or "pay off all credit cards." Calculate what you must do **every month** to reach these annual goals, then follow through.

9. Have an attorney prepare and update your will. Review titling of property (especially joint tenancies). As your financial situation improves, additional estate planning (including trusts) may become appropriate.

10. Adequately cover all your insurance needs (including life and disability income coverage). Review type of coverage, amounts and beneficiary designations with your agent every two years.

11. Try to obtain the right ratio of savings, insurance and investments. Have enough money in liquid assets for emergencies. Put remaining funds into **diversified** and well-researched investments. Be aware of all types of financial risks, not just investment risk. "Conservative" assets (CDs and money market funds) are vulnerable to interest rate risk and inflation risk, which can erode your buying power.

12. At the start of each new year, list the value of your assets and debts. Compare these to the prior year's figures to measure how well you are doing. Project what you'd like next year's amounts to be. Periodically graph or chart your liquid asset and debt situation. Become vigilant about your financial situation and motivate yourself to improve your financial situation. Doing all these things will not be easy, but if you can reach your goals, the rest of your life will be easier and more enjoyable.

BUILDING YOUR FINANCIAL CASTLE

WEALTH IS NOT HIS THAT HAS IT, BUT HIS THAT ENJOYS IT.
BENJAMIN FRANKLIN

In addition to the garden analogy, sometimes the financial planning process is like building a castle.

Though more noble projects dominate the lives of most people, one on-going goal we unconsciously strive toward is the construction of a good, solid, well-protected castle.

I'm not just referring to your home, whether it be a five-acre mansion with a view of the ocean and llamas grazing in your front yard or a VW bus with a psychedelic paint job. In this sense, your castle represents the accumulation of assets during your lifetime.

Most of us move away from our childhood home with no more belongings than it takes to fill a mid-sized compact car. Our financial assets at that time are even less significant.

We gradually acquire some financial assets: a small savings account, a retirement account at our first job, a mutual fund. At some point we begin to buy various types of insurance. Some are lucky enough to afford to buy a home. This building process continues until we retire, when this castle of assets is strong enough to provide us with a reasonable standard of living in our non-working years.

To achieve success, you must lay a good foundation. Then, you customize your castle to ensure that it is both functional and well-adapted to your personal style.

One hazard of successful castle building is this: the more attractive your castle becomes, the more vulnerable it becomes to financial marauders such as natural disasters, personal tragedies, job changes, sickness, death, disability, divorce and lawsuits. To discourage and deflect some of these challenges, you need to build a moat around the castle's perimeter. The modern version of the moat is called insurance.

You also need to be on the lookout for financial villains that threaten your castle: inflation, stock market declines, rising interest rates, changing tax laws, and general economic uncertainty.

Atop your castle, around the circumference, peering over the parapets, you position guards ready to fend off the intruders which may attack from any direction. There is no way to totally protect yourself and your castle from all these threats. All you can do is prepare well for the attack and minimize the damage if it occurs.

Many people are afraid of stock market crashes, so they have all their money in a savings account. They seek safety by putting all their guards on that side of the castle. You never really know what will threaten you next, so you must diversify, or spread your assets around the perimeter, so you can expand your castle while providing prudent protection.

If you look at your overall financial situation in this manner, you will continuously attempt to balance growth with protection. How to allocate your scarce resources between increasing your assets and protecting them is one of the toughest, on-going financial challenges you must face.

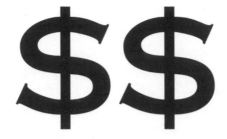

MONEY STRATEGIES

The following chapter discusses three of the most common dreams, and describes some simple concepts that can help motivate you to make sacrifices today to turn your dreams into realities tomorrow.

Pre-fund your dream vacation

Save before spending instead of charging and paying later

Does it bother you if you have to postpone your next vacation because you are still paying for the fading memories of the last one? This may not be too painful if that was a GREAT vacation, but if your fondest memories of that Caribbean cruise involved Hurricane Mildred, sweet purple rum drinks, and dancing too many Mambos with a swarthy rugby player from Argentina, it's better if the trip is paid for quickly.

You probably know where you want to take your next vacation, and you've got a good idea of when it will be, but do you know how much it will cost? Vacations almost always cost more than you anticipate. If you enjoy planning trip details—where to stay, what to wear, and what potency of sunscreen to bring—now is the time to create a budget and start saving. If you can't save enough, explore some options:

- scale down your plans,
- save more,
- postpone your trip, or
- decide how far into debt you are willing to go.

The example here shows how to reduce your vacation's cost by pre-funding it. The savings may even be enough to pay for a sky diving lesson or an extra day at your favorite posh resort. At the very least, you should be able to afford a few more purple rum drinks, an extra bottle of Dramamine, and some Mambo lessons.

Pre-Funding Your $5,000 Vacation Versus Charging It

PRE-FUNDING

Start saving this month. Deposit $405 per month into a special savings account, (6% interest assumed).

When you start your vacation in one year you will have **$5000**.

CREDIT CARD FINANCING

When you return home from your vacation in a year, begin paying $405 a month on the $5,000 balance on your 15% interest credit card.

Your trip won't be paid off for 14 months. Total cost is $5,468.

Extra amount to spend on your vacation = $468

College for $5 a day
Break massive goals into manageable commitments

For the cost of a cheap lunch, you can build a substantial college education fund for your child. If you invest $5 per day at an 8% rate of return, starting with the day your child is born, you will accumulate almost $90,000 by the time he or she is eighteen.

That's the good news. The bad news is that your stomach will be growling every afternoon for the next eighteen years. Also, according to the College Board, the cost of a four-year college education is projected to be $118,000 at a public school and $248,000 at a private school by 2013.

The point of this is not to discourage you from starting a college account for your child. It may seem nearly impossible to save for college, especially if you have more than one child, but by starting early and contributing often, you can build a sizable account. You'll be surprised how rapidly it grows.

The astronomical projections seem hard to believe, but should they prove accurate, your kids may need to make up the difference by working part-time or getting scholarships. Or your adult child could live at home until he or she is 23. Maybe you'd better save $10 a day.

Retirement
Start Early

"Retire" is a strange word. Most people don't want to tire, but they do want to retire. This magical vision haunts the lunchrooms of most companies. Depending where you work, retirement can become an obsession as early as age 22. Unfortunately, too many people talk about retirement and too few actively do something to make their retirement something more exciting than sitting in a lawn chair in the front yard watching cars drive by.

The secret to retiring early with enough money to enjoy your free time is to start when you are young—the earlier the better. The following chart shows how much you would have to save each month to have a million dollars by age 65. It is possible that by your retirement, your $1,000,000 will buy nothing more than a fancy lawn chair, so be sure to read the chapter on inflation.

How to become a millionaire by age 65

(Amount you must save **each month** to accumulate $1,000,000)

	Rate of Return	
Starting Age	6%	12%
25	$508	$97
35	$994	$308
45	$2,137	$1,033
55	$5,965	$4,241

One of the best things about saving for retirement is that the government actively encourages you to do so. When you put money into a qualified retirement plan through work, or when you fund your own retirement if you are self employed, you receive two types of tax benefits.

First, your contributions reduce current year taxes. Second, the earnings on those funds also grow tax-deferred, so they grow untaxed until withdrawn.

If living a comfortable retirement is a goal for you, you **must** sacrifice today. To pursue any dream, you **must** give up something TODAY to get something TOMORROW.

POWER OF DIVERSIFICATION

Several years ago, Sam and Kathy, a couple of my favorite clients, gave me a wonderful gift for Christmas—a blue sweatshirt with big letters across the front that said: "DIVERSIFY." That's when I knew I had made my point with them.

To me, diversification is something of a financial religion. If you learn nothing else from this book, let it be that you should put your money in a variety of places, and I don't mean Certificates of Deposit at three different banks.

One of the main things people seek in an investment is *safety*. For some people, this means putting your money in a federally insured savings account at a bank that for the last one hundred years has had the same name and is located across the street from your house. Ideally, this bank should also be surrounded by a high fence topped with jagged barbed wire and guarded at night by an irritable Doberman pinscher.

WALL STREET IS WHERE
THE PROPHETS TELL US
WHAT WILL HAPPEN AND
PROFITS TELL US WHAT DID
HAPPEN.

UNKNOWN

It is crucial to have a sufficient amount of cash to deal with emergencies and unexpected cash flow. You never know when you will unexpectedly need a large amount of money for a medical emergency, a major car repair or Rolling Stones concert tickets.

However, many people do themselves a disservice by placing their money only in savings accounts, Certificates of Deposit and bonds. Of course, if having your money anywhere else would drive you crazy, stop reading this book and reread the safety manual that came with your pillow.

Sorry, I know I'm being a smart aleck. I realize that lots of people are afraid of investments that can decrease in value. However, I'm con-

INVESTMENT OPTIONS

Stock: An equity-type investment or a share of ownership in a company. These investments are bought and sold on organized stock exchanges or "over-the-counter."

Bond: A debt-type investment. A security representing a loan to a company or government unit. Interest rates are specified as is the time period until repayment. Duration can range from one month to thirty years or more.

Mutual Fund: A flexible investment product that packages a variety of investments. Investment companies hire managers who select securities that match the goals which are defined in the fund prospectus. Stocks and bonds are purchased using a pool of money acquired from individual mutual fund investors. Advantages of mutual funds include: professional money management, quick liquidity should you wish to sell your shares, flexibility of investment types and the ease of purchase.

As of 1998, there are about 10,000 American mutual funds. Mutual funds can buy a variety of investments: big stocks, small stocks, foreign stocks, company bonds, government bonds, real estate, etc. Because of the infinite possible combinations of investments and strategies, mutual funds alone can provide tremendous diversification. They are the best way to start investing.

Money Market Fund: A type of mutual fund which invests in short-term bonds and securities. May be taxable or tax-free. Pays an interest rate that fluctuates daily.

vinced that in the long run, an investment that may decrease in value ultimately has a much better chance of increasing your money's **real** amount of buying power.

Investments such as bonds and money market funds are debt-related. You loan money to an institution in return for a specified or variable interest rate. Stocks and stock mutual funds are equity-based, meaning you own a small part of the companies in which you invest. If the companies prosper, your investment increases in value, but this potential for a higher return is linked to a greater risk of financial loss.

If you place your assets in a variety of locations, you increase the overall safety of your portfolio. Eventually you should have some money in cash, some in bonds, some in foreign investments, some invested in stocks of large companies, some in small company stocks, some in hard assets (such as gold), some in real estate… I could go on but I won't.

This approach is not necessarily the best way to maximize your investment return, but it is a good defensive strategy that also offers more potential for growth than debt-related investments alone.

Futures
Options
Commodities
Hard Assets
Emerging Market
Foreign Investments
Small Company Stocks
High Yield (Junk Bonds)
Large Company Stocks
Balanced Mutual Funds
Individual Bonds
Bond Mutual Funds
Government Bonds
Money Market Funds
Insured Bank Accounts and Certificates of Deposit

RISK

RETURN POTENTIAL

Pyramid of assets

In an earlier chapter, I talked about the castle of financial planning. Now I'm going to switch to The Great Pyramid of Risk analogy. In the chart below, the riskiest of assets are at the top and the most stable are at the bottom.

As you would expect, when building a stable pyramid you want to start with a large, sturdy foundation. Rather than beginning with the riskiest and most exciting investments, you need to start with the boring but predictable debt-related products. These liquid assets can be quickly and easily converted to cash.

As you will notice, the investments noted in the illustration become progressively "riskier" as you move higher up the pyramid. In constructing your personal pyramid you need to be aware of your risk tolerance. Even savvy investors reach a point where they choose not to build higher. The next level of investment, despite the greater potential for gain, is not necessarily worth the anxiety it produces.

If you are comfortable with greater investment risk, you may choose to skip entire levels of investments to seek a greater potential return. This, of course, increases your risk of loss if the investment turns sour.

Investments that have the greater return potential should be held over a longer period. Just like plants, they need time to grow.

No-Load Beer

A PENNY SAVED IS TWO PENCE CLEAR,
A PIN A DAY'S A GROAT A YEAR.
BENJAMIN FRANKLIN

A local tavern owner once told me she only bought no-load mutual funds; a radio financial expert advised her to do that. As we talked, I sipped my half pint of imported lager and, utilizing her philosophy, thought about the unsound economic decision her customers were making.

People visited her popular pub even though it was not the cheapest place in town to purchase a beer. Had her patrons considered only the price, they would have bought a six-pack of Generic No-Load Beer at their local discount liquor store and consumed it alone in their living rooms.

Her customers, however, obviously felt it was appropriate to pay more for the additional benefits: pleasant atmosphere, music, cheerful conversation, and the possibility of initiating a thoughtful, yet stimulating relationship with an attractive stranger.

Similarly, it's often worthwhile to pay a financial professional for his or her assistance. But when *Money Magazine* tells readers they are fools if they don't use no-load mutual funds, investors start to wonder whether they should take care of their own finances. After all, why would anyone pay sales charges, asset-based management fees, or hourly charges when all you have to do is buy some financial software, subscribe to a mutual fund rating service and dial up the Internet?

I used to save money by changing the oil in my old VW. Now I'd just as soon not climb under my car and get my hands dirty. The same philosophy applies to finances. Poor investments can be messier than a bucket of used motor oil. Many savvy investors spend more time reading the Wall Street Journal than I do, but others would rather tend to their gardens. Leisure time has value too.

I often ponder what it is I really get paid for. Usually I conclude that there's more to financial planning than picking a hot mutual fund. Just because a fund has four stars or five dollar signs or six happy faces doesn't mean it's the best fund for that particular individual at that time.

Occasionally the wise choice is to hang on to what appears to be a lousy fund; at other times it's best not to invest at all. Instead, it might be better to first pay off your credit cards, purchase an insurance policy, or build up an emergency cash fund.

For most people, it's hard to make investment decisions, especially when their cautious friends are flocking to CDs and the savvy investor they know is investing in Uruguayan utility funds. Advice from financial publications can add to the confusion. These periodicals know that a headline like *"Stick to your Long-term Objectives"* won't sell nearly as many magazines as *"Nine Naughty Funds for the Nineties."*

Sometimes, even conventional wisdom is wrong. In late 1994, after a rough year for the stock market, the vast majority of financial experts predicted a worse stock market in 1995. What followed were three of the best years in stock market history.

People don't necessarily mind paying more for certain services and products. A Rolex watch keeps time no better than does a Timex, and Buicks are cheaper than BMWs, but if consumers believe they receive additional value, they're willing to pay more.

Professional financial advice also doesn't come cheap, but if you don't have the time, talent or temperament for managing your investments, this may be money well spent.

Be a wise consumer. When you comparison shop for counsel regarding your financial future, you can't afford to look merely at the price. You can save money by mowing your own lawn, but it's advisable to hire an expert for tasks such as root canals and vasectomies. For tasks in between, weigh price against value, then decide.

CONSULTING WITH FINANCIAL ADVISORS

THERE ARE ONLY THREE KINDS OF PEOPLE: THOSE WHO CAN COUNT
AND THOSE THAT CAN'T.
BUMPER STICKER

Few financial advisors are fearsome creatures, but many people fear discussing their finances with others. Some clients are shy, if not out-right embarrassed, about discussing money matters if they fear they will appear ignorant. Individuals hate to admit that they have done a poor job of accumulating assets, despite having adequate income and living a comfortable lifestyle.

Money is a very private topic. According to Maria Nemeth, PhD, clinical psychologist and author of *You and Money: Would it be all Right With You if Life Got Easier?*, "Many of us would rather talk about our sex lives than discuss the paycheck we bring home each month."

When you decide to begin investing, one of the first decisions you need to make is whether to use a financial advisor or go it alone. Some people are "do-it-yourselfers" when it comes to handling money mat-ters. It's a challenging hobby that can bring pleasure and wealth. Not everyone needs the assistance of an advisor, but many wealthy investors eventually pay a professional for money management or financial advice.

A 1998 study by the International Association for Financial Planning and Boston-based research company DALBAR, Inc. concluded that, "Sixty-four percent of middle and high-income consumers pay professionals for advice." Additional findings showed that "forty-eight percent of individuals with $25,000 seek the help of a professional, while 70% of those with over $500,000 work with a professional."

If you are considering working with a financial planner or investment consultant, take the time to interview several. Ask friends for referrals. Determine if the services provided are worth the cost of the expertise and experience you'll receive. Initial consultations are often free.

Some categories of financial professionals, along with the accompanying acronyms they have earned, are noted in the glossary. Whether or not you hire someone is a decision to base on a variety of factors:

- your current level of financial expertise,
- amount of money you have to invest,
- the sophistication of your financial needs or goals, and
- whether you have the time and temperament to deal with these issues yourself.

The following list of questions may be helpful when interviewing an advisor:

1) How long have you been in this business?
2) How did you get into this business? What is your prior experience?
3) Why are you in this business?
4) What exactly do you do?
5) How do you get paid? How much do you charge?
6) Do you think that nose-ring really enhances your appearance?
7) How often will we meet?
8) What reports will you provide to me?
9) What is the nature of your professional training?
10) Do you hold any professional designations? What do those letters behind your name mean?

11) Do you belong to any professional organizations such as the IAFP, ICFP and CLU/ChFC Society?
12) Who played Mary Ann on Gilligan's Island?

(If the proposed financial advisor answers correctly*, politely excuse yourself and find a different advisor to interview.)

*Dawn Wells

What Services Does Professional Advice Provide?

If your primary need is implementing your investments, there are several options. The lowest cost option is to buy no-load mutual funds by calling an 800 telephone number or by trading stocks on the Internet. If you are a novice investor and are easily intimidated by financial jargon or suave bank tellers, this type of transaction may be unnerving.

When working with investment advisors, your most common choices involve:

- **Hourly consultation charges.** Paying for tax, financial or investment advice by the hour. If you develop a financial plan, there may be a flat charge for the entire project.
- **Asset-based management fees.** The advisor manages your investments and you regularly receive consolidated statements. Cost is from .5% to 3% of the assets under management. Higher fees usually indicate the use of a separate professional money manager to manage your individual stock portfolio. Minimum balance for most fee-based accounts can start as low as $20,000 but may be over $1,000,000.
- **Commission-based sales charges or loads.** Advisors receive compensation for advice from commissions generated by the investments recommended and implemented.

All mutual funds, even no-load funds, have internal operating expenses ranging from .5% to over 2% per year. This pays the salaries of the managers who select the stocks, prospectus and statement costs, and customer service expenses.

Types of load mutual fund shares

Mutual funds can employ a variety of sales charges, but the most common are noted below:

A shares - Up-front, one-time sales charge of 2-6%.

B shares - Rear-end sales charge paid only if that fund is sold during the surrender period (usually 5-8 years). Charge decreases each year and is based on the value of the account when the fund is sold.

C shares - There is no up-front or rear-end sales charge, but the annual charge or 12(b)1 fee is up to 1%. This is higher than the normal .25% annual "trail" commissions paid to the brokers.

NO-LOAD - No up-front loads, rear-end loads or 12(b)1 fees. Usually, no investment advice is provided unless you pay an advisor separately.

Which *type* of shares are appropriate for you depends on various factors, but the length of time you will hold your investment is very important.

The following chart shows what the value of an investment would be worth, factoring in the fees of various types of shares and the length of time held.

COMPARING IMPACT OF SALES CHARGES

	Original Investment $10,000			
	PURE NO-LOAD FUND	B SHARES BACK LOAD* FUND	A SHARES 4% FRONT END LOAD	A SHARES 4% FRONT END LOAD**
Projected Rate				
of Return	7%	7%	7%	8%
Amount Invested	$10,000	$10,000	$9,600	$9,600
Surrender Value				
In Three Years	$12,250	$11,838	$11,760	$12,093
In Five Years	$14,025	$13,885	$13,464	**$14,102**
In Ten Years	$19,672	$19,672	$18,884	**$20,725**
In Twenty Years	$38,697	$38,697	$37,149	**$44,737**

*No front-end load, but surrender charge that decreases over five years (5%, 4%, 3%, 2%, and 1% in fifth year and none thereafter)

** Assuming all alternatives have the same annual expense rate and that each earns exactly the same rate of return, the no-load fund will outperform the A and C shares. B shares will catch up to no-load shares when redemption charges disappear.

If, by using information from an advisor, you can increase your rate of return by just 1% per year, the A shares will start outperforming all other options after five years.

Using the services of a financial advisor will not necessarily help you to achieve a higher rate of return. There is no way to guarantee a higher return solely by investing in a no-load fund with the lowest fees *or* by hiring the most expensive advisor you can find.

My best service to clients has rarely been when I recommended a particular stock, industry or mutual fund. Helping clients generate the courage to start investing, then encouraging them to continue toward their goals, despite market fluctuations, is my most valuable function.

Often, my most valuable advice was when I told my clients to do nothing. I told them not to panic when the market got scary. I also told them not to borrow money to invest when the market was so good that losing money seemed unlikely.

My point is that sometimes investors become obsessed with minimizing fees and expenses, but with long-term investing, your discipline and the stock and mutual fund performance become more important factors. You may independently be able to find the key to successful investing, or you may want to work with a paid advisor to help you find the key.

Test Your Financial Knowledge

1) Which of the following $10,000 investments would accumulate a higher value after 5 years?

A-   Year 1 UP 30%,
      Year 2 UP 30%,
      Year 3 Down 20%,
      Year 4 UP 30%,
      Year 5 Down 20%.

B - Steady 8% per year increase.

2) If a $10,000 investment increased by 50% in Year 1 and decreased 50% in year 2, what would be its value?

A - $12,500.

B - $7, 500.

C - $10,000.

3) Which $10,000 invested would be worth more after 10 years?

A - An 8% per year investment which deducted a one-time up-front 5% sales charge.

B - An 8% per year investment which charged a 1% per year management fee at the end of each year.

C - A 7% per year investment which had no initial sales charge and no management fee.

CULTIVATING PATIENCE
(Hitchhiking and the Art of Investing)

THE WORST THING (ABOUT) THE MUTUAL FUND
INDUSTRY IS THE TENDENCY OF MONEY TO POUR INTO
FUNDS AT HIGHS AND POUR OUT AT THE LOWS.
JOHN BOGLE, CEO OF VANGUARD GROUP OF INVESTMENT COMPANIES

"Patience is a virtue." My wife and I recently recalled a scene from our 1975 cross-country adventure. That summer we had left our car at home and traveled 15,000 miles around the U.S. and Canada using various forms of transportation. One third of that mileage was completed by hitchhiking.

At one point, we were stranded next to Interstate 90 in Wyoming, just east of the Continental Divide. We were wearing every item of clothing we carried, but it kept getting colder. We could actually hear a car or truck approaching well before we saw it; two minutes later it would pass us by. Each time a car failed to pick us up we reminded each other: "Patience is a virtue."

It was true. There was absolutely nothing we could do until the next car passed by. After what seemed like two hours, a pick-up truck stopped. We threw our backpacks in the back, then rode over the pass and down the road another hundred miles.

What does this have to do with investing? Everything. This age of urgency breeds impatience: at stop lights, in grocery checkout lines, at ATM's, on the Internet and as we monitor our investments. Despite committing to a "five year or longer" investment strategy, financial publications tend to focus on short-term performance. If your fund only got two stars while many others got four or five, there is a natural temptation to switch to a fund with more stars. Sometimes this works—and sometimes it doesn't.

At a 1996 conference I was sitting next to the manager of a prominent values-based mutual fund. He was there to talk about his evolution from media darling, based on stellar performance in the early 1990s, to a fund manager pariah who was now ignored because his fund had seriously underperformed in the market for two consecutive years. I liked him and had always had great faith in his stock-picking skills, so I never suggested that my clients move to a different fund. I'm glad I was patient; during the next year his fund was again a top-performing fund.

If you are investing for the long-term, it is essential to not switch funds too frequently. So, whether you are becoming impatient with a mutual fund or that chatty bank teller, remember that patience is a very valuable utensil to keep in your emotional tool box.

PROTECTING
YOUR CROPS

As your money crops begin to germinate you will be confronted with a variety of threats and obstacles. You may even consider delaying or abandoning your dreams. Try not to let this happen.

Many threats and obstacles can be anticipated; others are unexpected and unlikely. Your greatest barriers, however, may be the ones you create. To surmount these self-imposed barriers, you must be willing to change personal habits. Only by gaining a greater awareness of these adversaries can you minimize their impact on your financial dreams.

THE GREATEST THREAT

ERE YOU CONSULT YOUR FANCY, CONSULT YOUR PURSE.
BENJAMIN FRANKLIN

There is one massive obstacle that prevents many people from living their dreams. It may be an obvious nemesis, but I must state it clearly: ***You Spend Too Much Money.***

The second most common response to my words of wisdom is, "I can't spend any less than I already do." The most frequent response is a short epithet that reflects negatively on my heritage.

Maybe you aren't an excessive spender, but most people do spend too much on immediate Wants, as opposed to Needs. It's hard to kick frivolous spending using the "cold-turkey" method, and if you are too harsh with yourself, you will soon rebel.

One of the best techniques to keep rebellion from happening is to give yourself an allowance. Every month, or every paycheck, give yourself a certain amount of money. Immediately separate it from your normal stash of cash, then keep it in a special place.

How much you give yourself is up to you, but the important thing is that this is YOUR money for your special indulgences. If you are married or in a relationship where you pool your funds, each of you should get an allowance. This technique can allow guilt-free golf playing.

Naturally, you can't use your "normal money" to pay for most indulgences anymore. Don't get carried away with definitions here, but do remember that *you* determine whether or not *you* are playing by the rules.

It might surprise you that by spending less, you'll accumulate enough in your special fund to buy indulgences that you might otherwise not have been able to afford.

LEARNING TO USE RISK
What chances should you take with your money?

THE DAY THE STOCK MARKET CRASHED IN 1987, I WENT FROM HAVING A
MILLION DOLLARS TO LESS THAN A HUNDRED THOUSAND. BUT DO YOU KNOW
HOW MUCH ATTENTION I GAVE IT? ONE HOUR. DID I MAKE IT BACK? MANY
TIMES OVER.
DEEPAK CHOPRA QUESTIONED IN MONEY MAGAZINE

Marketing experts tell us that "safety" is one of those special words
which cause most people to respond positively. It is natural to be protective of your money; you work hard to earn it and work just as hard
to keep it. To be financially successful, however, you not only need to
accumulate money, you must then use it to grow more.

Referring back to the garden analogy, you wouldn't hide all of your
seeds in a safe deposit box just because some might die when you plant

them. It gives you much more pleasure to plant them and watch the crop flourish. Similarly, the fruits of your gardening efforts are not meant to be saved, they're meant to be consumed. I wouldn't recommend saving every tomato and banana you grow.

Novice investors are often tempted to be too cautious with hard-earned or inherited money. Yet practicing "safe investing" sometimes is more harmful to long-term financial health than catching the investment fever.

Most people think the only financial risk is **market risk**—when the value of your investment goes up and down. This is the most obvious type of risk. In fact it is quantified daily in the financial section and on the local news. In reality, other types of risk can sometimes be just as hazardous.

I FINALLY KNOW WHAT DISTINGUISHES MAN FROM THE OTHER BEASTS: FINANCIAL WORRIES.

JULES RENARD

Here are some of the most common types of risk.

- **Inflation Risk** - This is the least perceivable type of risk. Your bank book shows a larger balance at the end of the year, but you have less buying power.
- **Interest Rate Risk** - When investing in bonds or other interest-related investments, the value of your original investment can fluctuate based on whether current interest rates go higher or lower.
- **Concentration Risk** - This happens when your mind drifts and you don't pay enough attention to your investments. Actually, this occurs when too much of a portfolio is in one stock or category of investment. The best way to protect yourself is by diversifying assets: putting them into a variety of investments that react differently to various negative economic circumstances.
- **Longevity Risk** - If you live *too* long, you run out of money and/or earning power. This isn't a bad risk when you consider the alternative. Like most risks, it's one we must live with.
- **Currency Risk** - Potential loss or gain can result from investing in foreign companies and countries. Changes in exchange rates between currencies create additional fluctuations in your investment value.
- **Credit Risk** - Default or delayed payment can happen when investing in loans, bonds or bond mutual funds.

- **Tax or Regulatory Risk** - Congress may change laws or eliminate tax benefits of a particular investment.
- **Event Risk** - An unexpected event can impact the value of a particular company or industry.
- **Economic Risk** - Prices may fluctuate based on large scale events that impact the entire economy rather than just an individual company.

There are several other types of risk, but I've probably made you too paranoid already. Total avoidance of all types of risk is impossible. Now that you have all these new risks to worry about, you may be tempted to do nothing, but the value of your money will still be at risk.

TIME REDUCES RISK AND INCREASES RETURN POTENTIAL

Which is the riskiest investment: stocks, bonds or U.S. Treasury Bills? Logic says that stocks are the riskiest. Stocks fluctuate the most, particularly over one-year time periods, but when you look at a twenty-year period of time, the statistics show that the potential for greater return is often worth the additional risk of stocks.

Ibbotson Associates, in their *Stocks, Bonds, Bills and Inflation 1998 Yearbook*, measured returns from various investment vehicles. Maximum and minimum rates of return were compared over 1, 5, 10, 15 and 20-year rolling time periods between 1925 and 1997.

Here are some random statistics concerning short-term versus long-term performance:
- The highest one-year return for small stocks was 143% in 1933. This volatile category lost 58% of its value in 1937. It's best twenty year return was 21% per year; the worst was 6%.
- U.S. Treasury bills, traditionally considered to be one of the safest investments, had their best year in 1981 at 15%. Throughout most of the 1930s and 1940s, their yields averaged only about 1%. Over all twenty year period, the best rate of return for T-bills was 8%, slightly ahead of the worst twenty year period for small stocks.
- Value in 1997 of $100 invested in various investment categories in 1977:

  U.S. Treasury Bills - $157

  Long-term government bonds - $278

  Large company stocks - $838

  Small company stocks - $1,001

NOTE: Historical comparisons can be helpful, but avoid translating such statistics into assurances that the future will behave similarly.

Don't Give Yourself Credit

No gain is so certain as that which proceeds from the economical use
of what we already have.
Latin Proverb

Don't give yourself too much credit, even if credit card companies are willing to.

Almost all financial problems result from the Primary Law of Personal Economics: No one has enough money. There are two responses to this Economic Law. Strategy #1—do not buy things unless you have the money to pay for them. Strategy #2— purchase what you want now and worry about how to pay for it later.

As long as you have discipline and don't get carried away, Strategy #2 can work, but if discipline is not an attribute you possess, the consequences can be dire.

Generally speaking, the more credit cards you carry, the more likely you are to be heavily in debt. A key warning signal is when you charge a special backpack to transport all of your credit cards.

Credit card dependence is one of the toughest addictions to kick. You undoubtedly receive unsolicited credit applications and pre-approved cards. How long would a heroin junkie stay clean if he received syringes in his mail several times a week?

If you have tried everything and believe your situation is out of control, it may be time to talk to a professional financial advisor or credit counselor. Credit problems are not insurmountable. Here are some simple strategies you can use to get control of your finances.

Throw a Credit Card Party

If you have reached the point where you know credit cards are your enemies, it's time to have a party. All family members who use the cards must attend. If you know of friends in a similar situation, invite them too.

Bring these things to the party:
- All your credit cards.
- Recent monthly bills showing interest rate, outstanding balance, annual fee, minimum monthly payment and the phone number of the company that issued the card.
- Scissors, hedge trimmers or other cutting instrument.
- A bottle of very expensive, well-aged Cabernet you just charged. Just kidding. Pay cash for a cheap but pleasant tasting table white, perhaps one with just a hint of nutmeg and a dash of broccoli. A non-alcoholic party beverage of your choice may be substituted.

DEBT IS THE WORST POVERTY.

THOMAS FULLER

Start gradually. Lay everything on the table in front of you. Sip your drink and chat with your cards. Share memories of some painful debts you've incurred together: nearly forgotten meals, that 110% polyester, powder-blue leisure suit, and wedding gifts to couples who are already divorced. Progressively work yourself into a frenzy. You can use salty language—you thought these nasty credit cards were your friends, but they are really your enemies, blocking your path to financial freedom.

When you are thoroughly enraged by their betrayal, kill them. Slice them up until they are nothing but little plastic rectangles, triangles and rhombuses. Show no mercy. Make this a vivid visual experience that you can recall to help you resist temptation years from now.

That's the easy and fun part. Now, call each company that issued the card; cancel the card and tell their courteous representative not to send you a new one.

With your list of bills in front of you, prioritize how you will pay them off. Choose the one with the highest interest rate or lowest outstanding balance. Pay off this one quickly. Make the minimum payment on all others, then choose your next victim.

I suggest sparing one low-interest credit card. Use this JUST for emergencies and for identification when renting a car. Describe in writing what you define to be an emergency and wrap this note around your card. Store the card in a place other than your wallet.

Review your progress periodically. If you are doing well, congratulate yourself and pay cash to buy yourself a minor reward. If you can defeat these fearsome enemies, you deserve compensation.

Freeze Your Credit

One way to avoid impulsive spending is to put your lone credit card in a plastic glass, fill it with water and put it in your freezer. If you have the urge to use it, you must wait until the ice melts. By then the impulse may be gone. Important note: microwaves may not be used.

When to Use Credit

If you know you need to limit your spending, place yourself on a cash basis immediately. This means, "If you don't have the cash, don't buy it." Use debt sparingly, or not at all. If you do charge something, pay the bill in full as soon as it comes.

Buying a personal residence requires getting into big-time debt, but the tax and investment advantages are offsetting factors. The need to purchase a different car or a major appliance may be a compelling enough reason to use debt. You should strive to totally avoid using credit for meals and small purchases until you have your finances under control again.

Also, check out your options on consolidating your debt into one loan, but look carefully at the fees, interest rates and the total amount you will be paying with a longer-term loan. Be a good consumer when analyzing your options. Don't delay dealing with the problem or you will sink deeper into debt over time.

Get outside help

If your situation is too overwhelming to tackle alone, ask a friend for a referral to a financial advisor, or try a non-profit credit counselor such as those affiliated with Consumer Credit Counseling Services. The sooner you realize you have a serious problem, the sooner you will be able to confront it, pay off your Past Self and get back on the road toward your dream.

NEVER FORGET: Once you are out of consumer debt, don't let it happen again.

CAR WARS
(Mode of transportation or object of envy)

THIS IS THE ONLY COUNTRY THAT EVER WENT TO THE
POORHOUSE IN AN AUTOMOBILE.
WILL ROGERS, EARLY 1930s

Fasten your seat belts, you are in for some warp-speed ranting and raving.

Since we're talking about spending less money, allow me to bring up one of my pet peeves: cars.

Except for credit card abuse, cars destroy more financial dreams than any other contributing factor. Most of the time, drivers aren't even aware of this. NOTE: If your primary dream is to own a purple Z23 Turbo Porsche, skip this chapter. It will offend you.

I freely admit that I am prejudiced in this area. Take what I say with a cup of salt, but don't entirely discount what I say. To me, cars are a means of transportation, a way of getting from Point A to Point B (or Fresno if you don't know anyone in Point B).

Cars are much more important to others than to me. My Mercury Zephyr Z7 is over twenty years old. I think of it as a classic; my wife and kids think of it as an eyesore, but it does get me to work and back with a minimum of expense and inconvenience.

HE IS RICHEST WHO IS CONTENT WITH THE LEAST, FOR CONTENT IS THE WEALTH OF NATURE.

SOCRATES

It isn't that I can't afford a newer car, it's just that I hate spending money on car payments. It may not surprise you, after reading this far, that I am occasionally accused of being stingy.

My feelings about cars, however, arise from knowing too many clients whose beautiful cars are fully equipped with large five-year loans. The left front tire of some vehicles cost more than the Blue Book value of my Zephyr. I'm being judgmental again, but good money management is at least partially about having your priorities in order.

Jonathan Pond, the well-known financial commentator and author of *The New Century Family Money Book*, released a study in 1995 that shows how costly Americans' love affairs with automobiles can be.

Based on the assumptions used in his study, "A person who trades an average-priced car every ten years will save enough money to be able to retire five years sooner than those who trade their cars every three years." The study continues, "In 40 years a person who holds onto a car for ten years will have approximately $385,000 more savings than the person who trades or leases a car every three years."

I'm not recommending a 1978 Mercury Zephyr to everyone. I'm just saying you should consider alternative ways to spend your money the next time you want to buy a car. Safety and dependability are crucial, but not everyone needs to own a new vehicle that is capable of crossing the Colorado River during a torrential storm.

Try to minimize your emotional response and be as pragmatic with this decision as you would with any other financial decision of this magnitude. Then don't let a stylish car drive you to the poor house.

SUCCESS CAN BE TAXING

I'M PROUD TO BE PAYING TAXES IN THE UNITED STATES.
THE ONLY THING IS, I COULD BE JUST AS PROUD FOR HALF THE MONEY.
ARTHUR GODFREY

Once you transcend the monetary survival stage of your financial life and enter the accumulation stage, a primary preoccupation becomes avoiding, delaying, and reducing tax bills. Some people even cheat on their taxes.

Our bizarre form of income tax collection significantly reduces our ability to accumulate assets. A small industry helps you minimize your contribution toward running our government. This includes: tax preparers, investment counselors, retirement consultants, and trust attorneys.

Our income tax system is progressive in nature. This means that the higher your income, the greater the percentage of your income goes to the government—in theory. A single taxpayer with no dependents who made $20,000 in 1997 paid 10% (or $2,000.00) of her income in taxes.

If she made $60,000, she would pay almost $12,000 (or 20%).

Once you accumulate a substantial sum of assets, however, you are better able to beat the tax game, thanks to our arbitrary tax system.

Another problem with our current income tax system is that it's just too easy for people to cheat. Just as with insurance and golf, the honest continuously subsidize the dishonest.

There are various strategies to legally avoid paying taxes on current income and defer the taxable income into future years.

THE INCOME TAX HAS MADE MORE LIARS OUT OF THE AMERICAN PEOPLE THAN GOLF HAS.

WILL RODGERS,
ILLITERATE DIGEST

Tax-Free Income

A common tax reduction strategy is to invest in tax-free municipal bonds. These are loans to local and state governments to finance public projects such as education, recreation, infrastructure, and giant plastic water slides.

The interest rate paid on these is usually **lower** than on taxable bonds, but as you can see in the next chart, if you are in a high tax bracket, your **after-tax** return could be higher. For example, if you earn a substantial income and are in the 39.6% federal tax bracket, a 5% **tax-free** bond yields the taxable equivalent of 8.2%.

However, don't get too obsessed with tax-free interest. If you are in the 15% tax bracket a 7% **tax-free** bond will produce less **after** tax income than a bond yielding more than 8.2%.

Taxable vs. Tax-Free interest
(Assumes Federal Income Tax Only)

TAX-FREE Yield of	5%	7%
	Will Equal a TAXABLE Yield of:	
Federal Tax Tax Rate		
15%	5.9%	**8.2%**
28%	6.9%	9.7%
39.6%	**8.2%**	11.6%

Tax Reduction by Deduction

The most common way taxpayers reduce their taxes is by spending money on items Congress declares are tax-deductible:

- Home interest
- Certain taxes
- Charitable contributions
- Significant medical expenses
- Some work related expenses

Entire books are written about tax deductions, so I'll only note how valuable deducting home mortgage interest can be. Essentially, the tax system subsidizes your purchase of an asset that hopefully will appreciate in value.

Keep in mind that when an expense is tax-deductible it does not mean it is **free**. The item simply costs less "after tax" than a non-deductible purchase. It is inadvisable to spend money for an item you don't need just because it is tax-deductible.

Deferring Income

Income taxes may be reduced by deferring *earned* income to a future tax year. The term "earned income" describes the money earned for doing physical or mental labor. This broad definition even includes wages earned when providing financial advice. Unearned income, by contrast, is generated by money or investments: interest, dividends and capital gains from stock sales.

Retirement plans, pensions, 401(k)s, 403(b)s, and Individual Retirement Accounts (IRAs) are the most common way to defer earned income. Once money is contributed into a retirement account, the tax on those earnings is also deferred until taken out. Like many benefits the government provides, these benefits are double-edged swords. Generally, you are penalized if you withdraw the money before you are 59^1/$_2$.

THE BEST THING TO SPEND ON YOUR CHILDREN IS YOUR TIME.

ARNOLD GLASGOW

When money is invested outside of a protected retirement account, earnings (interest from a savings account or the dividends from a mutual fund) are taxed each year—even if the money remains in the account.

Another investment tool for deferring tax on unearned income is the annuity. The original amount invested, the principal, is not tax deductible, but earnings are not taxed until withdrawn.

There are two basic kinds of annuities. Fixed annuities behave in a way similar to savings accounts that earn a specific interest rate for a certain period of time. Variable annuities act more like mutual funds—funds within separate investment accounts are used to purchase stocks and bonds.

Roth IRAs

While I was writing this book, a new tax-favored product was created by Congress—-the Roth IRA. Unlike traditional IRAs, which defer current earned income until money is withdrawn, Roth IRAs offer no *immediate* tax benefit. However, if certain conditions are met, money withdrawn from Roth IRAs is not taxed at all. This *may* be much more beneficial for your future situation than receiving an immediate tax break.

Appreciating Assets

Another way to postpone paying taxes on your investments is by purchasing property such as land or stocks. The value of these assets will fluctuate up and down, but the appreciation or gain in value is not taxed until that asset is sold. A stock you bought at $10 a share that is now worth $20 a share will not be taxed until it is sold. When stocks, bonds and certain other assets are sold, the gain is taxed at a lower tax rate if the assets have been held eighteen months or longer.

Income Shifting
Ugly Acronyms Can Help Fund College

One common way to save for your child's college expenses is to gift money or an asset to your minor son or daughter. Using a Uniform

Gift to Minors Act Account (UGMA) or Uniform Transfer to Minors Act Account (UTMA) is an inexpensive and uncomplicated strategy.

UTMAs and UGMAs can be used with a savings account, mutual fund or almost any asset. Funds placed into such an account become an irrevocable gift to your child that can not then be used for your normal parental responsibilities.

Care should be taken using UTMAs and UGMAs because once your child reaches age 18 (or up to 21 in some states), your child may use these funds as he or she pleases. Income generated in the child's accounts is usually taxed at a lower rate than funds in the parents' account. Be cautious, as UTMAs and UGMAs may eventually affect your child's ability to obtain college financial aid or need-based scholarships.

This chapter has discussed only the most common income tax reduction strategies. Books abound concerning reducing income tax and dealing with the tax consequences of certain financial decisions.

However, paying less in taxes shouldn't necessarily be your prime goal. How much you keep *after* paying taxes is where your focus should lie.

Would you rather earn $10,000 and pay no income tax or earn $100,000 and pay $40,000 in taxes?

WORK WELL WITH YOUR TAX ADVISOR: 10 TIPS

Few things are worse in the financial world than writing a check to the Internal Revenue Service. One of them is having to pay someone to calculate how much you must pay in taxes.

The Tax Code, as concocted by Congress and enforced by the IRS, is a bubbling stew created from federal budget requirements, political payoffs and economic theories. This set of regulations is so lengthy and complicated

TAX TIP

When writing a check to the IRS, spell out "Internal Revenue Service." "IRS" can be easily changed to "MRS. Jones." Also, put your Social Security number on all checks and correspondence.

that many intelligent and reasonable people must seek assistance to deal with the sadistic maze.

During the twenty-five years I've prepared taxes and chatted with accountants at tax seminars, I've compiled a list of suggestions for clients. These tips can help you select and work well with your tax advisor.

1) Meet with a tax preparer in February or March. At that point we still have most of our wits about us. Despite our calm and professional demeanor, most of us work way too many hours. If you wait until April, you will be dealing with an accountant who has been burning the candle at both ends and is just about out of wick.

I'm something of a slacker since I work only 60-70 hours a week during tax season. Still, too many of my late evenings are spent reviewing returns at home listening to scratchy Rolling Stones albums. For other preparers it may be Rosemary Clooney compact discs, but none of our clients would be comforted to see us just about midnight in early April.

2) Make appointments early in the day. Regardless of how committed your tax preparer is, working 10 straight hours with only two Milky Way breaks makes accountants cranky. When seeing his or her family awake becomes more important than finding an additional $100 deduction for you, your hard-earned money may become merely a number on a calculation sheet.

> TAXES ARE WHAT WE PAY FOR A CIVILIZED SOCIETY.
>
> JUDGE OLIVER WENDELL HOLMES, JR.

3) Look beyond prowess with an adding machine. Discretion should rank high among the characteristics you seek. Your tax return provides a wealth of personal information. In addition to your occupation, salary, and number of children, we know which charities you contribute to (or if you only donate that same $500 bag of old clothes each year). We also know if there was a major family illness, a refinanced mortgage or a contemplated divorce. We're also privileged to share the sordid details of that incredibly imprudent investment you never even told your golfing partners about.

4) Value honesty and attitude. Choose your accountant the way you would choose a physical therapist or roofing contractor. You may regret it if you choose the cheapest, but paying an exorbitant fee won't necessarily buy competence.

Avoid preparers who promise a massive refund or specialize in inventing creative yet credible deductions. If you get audited, you are the one who pays the tax, interest and penalties. By the time of your audit, your "tax professional" may be preparing tax returns in Costa Rica.

5) Tax preparation is an art, not a science. Science deals with the predictable and immutable laws of nature; income tax laws are created by legislators, enforced by bureaucrats and interpreted by judges. So find someone who is more than a technician.

6) Beware of a preparer who knows everything about taxes. Some tax questions just don't have an obvious answer. It is not uncommon to encounter dilemmas that our portly Tax Code book, computer software, and rows of reference guides don't even acknowledge. When certifiable answers do not exist, tax veterans understand the art of "tax logic."

All accountants have normal clients with weird tax situations, so, don't be overly concerned if your advisor can't answer every question immediately. We also have weird clients with normal tax situations, but I won't go into that.

7) Don't be petrified by the prospect of an audit. If you have a legitimate deduction, use it. The odds of being audited are only about one to two per cent for people with simple tax returns. But even if you are audited, it is unlikely that you will be dealing with a sadistic ogre.

8) Get organized. Accountants and accountant-types derive a perverse satisfaction from creating order out of confusion, but chaos disturbs us. Being organized may not only reduce your tax preparation bill, it will make your tax appointment more cordial—and less expensive.

9) Find someone who uses a computer or computer service to prepare your return. There are infinite ways to make dumb mistakes on a tax return. Computers excel at catching dumb mistakes.

However, don't be content with your return just because it was printed by a laser printer. Neatness is not a substitute for correctness. Double check your return and ask your preparer to explain anything that doesn't look correct.

10) Finally, whether you work with an accountant or not, don't habitually file extensions. If you can't get it together by April 15th, you probably won't have it together by August 13th, two days before the four-month extension expires.

Fortunately, not all tax preparers become so traumatized. While you should avoid tax preparers who work way too hard, such an advisor might be preferable to one who asks if you'd like him to clean out your rain gutters when he finishes preparing your return.

GOOD BUSINESSES IN AN INFLATIONARY ECONOMY

INFLATION

PERCENTAGE CHANGE DURING 1993 IN THE INFLATION RATE IN SERBIA,
+363,000,000,000,000,000%
HARPERS, INC. 1994

Inflation, I believe, is the greatest uncontrollable threat to almost everyone's money. If the economy experiences a significant level of inflation for a number of years, it will eat into the buying power of those assets you've worked very hard to build.

You can control many of the factors that determine your financial success, but other factors, such as inflation, are totally out of your control. All you can do is try to minimize the impact of inflation on your money.

As a kid, I remember paying a nickel for a candy bar the size of a small suitcase. This sounds like one of those legends parents are fond

HISTORY OF REAL RATE OF RETURN

	YIELD 3 MONTH T BILLS	AFTER TAX YIELD (35%)	COST OF LIVING (INFLATION)	REAL% RATE RETURN
1997	5.0	3.3	(1.7)	1.6
1996	5.0	3.3	(3.3)	0
1995	5.5	3.6	(2.5)	1.1
1994	4.2	2.7	(2.7)	0
1993	3.0	2.0	(2.7)	(0.7)
1992	3.5	2.3	(2.9)	(0.6)
1991	5.4	3.5	(3.1)	(3.1)
1990	7.5	4.9	(6.1)	(1.2)
1989	8.1	5.3	(4.6)	.7
1988	6.7	4.4	(4.4)	0
1987	5.8	3.8	(4.4)	(0.6)
1986	6.0	3.9	(1.1)	2.8
1985	7.6	4.9	(3.8)	1.1
1984	9.6	6.2	(3.9)	2.3
1983	8.6	5.6	(3.8)	1.8
1982	10.7	7.0	(3.9)	4.1
1981	14.0	9.1	(8.9)	.2
1980	11.5	7.5	(12.4)	(4.9)
1979	10.0	6.5	(13.3)	(6.8)
1978	7.2	4.7	(9.0)	(5.3)

SOURCE: "ECONOMIC INDICATORS," COUNCIL OF ECONOMIC ADVISORS, MARCH 1998

of telling, like when I used to walk to school through the Los Angeles snow – uphill — both ways. Over time, however, inflation's capacity to erode buying power can be dramatic.

The Shrinking Money Chart shows the diminishing buying power of a dollar. It's hard to believe, but it's true. You wouldn't doubt a chart, would you?

Inflation is particularly harmful to the process of financial planning because it is so devious. Many people who are afraid to invest in the stock market ignore the impact of inflation. Their $10,000 Certificate of Deposit (CD) at the bank that earns 5% will grow to $10,500 by the end of the year, but that amount may only purchase $9,800 worth of goods if the inflation rate is 7%.

The History of Real Rate of Return chart shows the annual rate of return on 3-month Treasury Bills *after* the impact of taxes and inflation. As you can see, this rate of return can vary dramatically from year to year. In 1995 for instance, the return on safe investments like a 3 month T-Bill was **5.5%**. After deducting an assumed 35% state and federal tax rate, the after-tax rate of return was **3.6%**. Since inflation that year was only 2.5%, the after tax and inflation rate of return was a positive **1.1%**.

In 1980, however, if you invested in a T-Bill yielding 11.5% (more than twice the 1995 rate), your buying power actually lost **4.9%**.

I often talk to older clients who are nostalgic for 1980 when they could earn 11.5% on their CD. Unless they locked in those rates for a long period of time, however, many don't recall that their buying power significantly shrank that year due to inflation.

Position your assets to take advantage of high interest rates if they start to rise, but be aware that over time, by locking in fixed rates, you are making that asset more vulnerable to inflation.

SHRINKING MONEY CHART

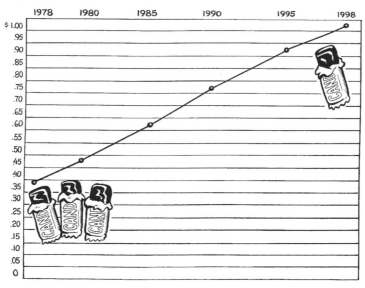

FEAR OF INSURANCE AGENTS

Warning: This chapter concerns scary stuff: death, disability, insurance and snakes. Though you may not want to read about insurance, you owe it to yourself and your loved ones to make mature judgments about this boring, but important topic.

People don't like to acknowledge their own mortality. In fact, death is the third greatest human fear, ranking just behind public speaking and meeting with life insurance agents. I felt the same way before I became an insurance agent twenty years ago. Once I started selling life insurance, I knew some of my clients were scared of me.

If the thought of insurance gives you the willies, this chapter may help desensitize you, reducing your fears to a more reasonable level. I have an unfounded fear of snakes. Despite what they taught you in Psychology 1A, what you're thinking is not true. To deal with my fear, I always force myself to visit the reptile house when I go to the zoo. My self-imposed therapy has desensitized me so well that I no longer need to watch where I step when I'm in airports and shopping malls.

LIFE INSURANCE

Even masochists don't like paying for life insurance, but if there are family members or others who are financially dependent upon you, your willingness to consider insurance coverage is a responsible and unselfish thing to do.

Life insurance serves the following purposes:
- Reduces financial stress at a time of great emotional upheaval,
- Provides cash to pay final expenses, probate costs, and estate taxes,
- Keeps your survivors from having to sell investments at an inopportune time,
- Allows you to fulfill plans such as sending your children to college, and
- Provides you with peace of mind.

How Much Life Insurance Should You Have?

Ask a dozen financial planners and life insurance agents to calculate the proper amount of life insurance you need and you'll receive twelve different answers.

If you are single with no dependents, no debts and some savings, you don't need life insurance unless you are protecting your insurability for the future by purchasing financial protection while you are in good health.

Three to five times your annual income will usually provide your survivors with enough money to survive a transition period while adapting to a new life if you die prematurely.

Most agents calculate life insurance need based on a total of the following amounts:
- Home mortgage balance. Paying this off, however, may not be a prudent tax and financial move, but it's a handy rule of thumb,
- Loans and credit card balances,
- Amount needed to provide a college fund for each child, and
- A lump sum of money large enough to generate interest to replace any remaining shortfall in income for the remainder of a partner's lifetime.

From this total you subtract any existing life insurance provided through your employer and any which you personally own.

The product of this formula is often startling. Amounts of half a million to a million dollars are not uncommon, yet the average size of a life insurance policy is $306,900 for men and $165,000 for women, according to LIMRA International, an insurance marketing and research association.

Your next step is to find out how much such coverage would cost. If you can't afford as much as you need, at least buy what you can afford.

What type of coverage should you buy?

This issue can become so confusing that it keeps some people from buying needed coverage.

• **Term Life Insurance** is like most types of insurance. It only pays off if the event that you are insuring against actually happens. Life insurance, however, is different from most other types of insurance because as you grow older, the likelihood of death increases.

According to actuarial charts, there is about a 5% probability a person will die in their seventieth year. A twenty year old male is thirty times less likely to die before his next birthday.

Term insurance rates go up annually, or every five, ten or twenty years, depending on the policy. The biggest problem with term insurance is that it rarely pays off. People tend to drop the coverage as they enter their fifties and sixties when the coverage becomes extremely expensive.

Compared to other types of life insurance, term insurance is like renting a house versus buying. The cost is much cheaper, but there is no savings component. Term insurance works best for most situations, but may not work well for long-term or permanent needs, such as estate planning.

• **Whole Life Insurance** solves the problem of rates increasing over time, but it is quite expensive. This is a fixed premium product that builds up a tax-deferred "cash value" that can be borrowed against. The initial premiums for whole life, however, can be five to fifteen times the cost of a term policy. Over time, the accumulated cash value decreases your net cost. This type of policy works best if you have a long-term need of twenty years or more or need estate tax protection if you have a substantial sum of assets.

- **Universal Life.** This product was developed in the early 1980s when interest rates were high. If you pay enough in premium, and the account earns enough interest over time, the account value should be able to subsidize the higher cost of insurance as you get older. The greatest advantage of this product is flexibility. Problems can arise at later ages if the interest earned is not enough to pay higher insurance rates in your sixties and beyond.
- **Variable Universal Life** is similar to Universal Life but instead of earning interest, the additional investment portion of the premium buys mutual fund-like assets. Obviously this works well when the stock market is doing well, but can have unpleasant consequences if the stock market performs poorly.

Determine the amount of coverage you need first, then decide what type you want and can afford. If you are uncertain what to do, buy term insurance with a quality company. You can always convert or change to a more permanent type of coverage.

Your ultimate decision may be complicated by the fact that every insurance agent believes he is the most honest, works for the most stable company and sells the finest product.

Some life insurance questions to ask:

- Which company? Stability should be considered as important an issue as cost. A variety of insurance rating services, including BEST, Standard and Poor's, Moody's, Duff & Phelps and Weiss Ratings give insurance companies a grade for stability.
- Which agent?
- Who should own the policy?
- Who should be the beneficiary?
- Would you prefer a paper or plastic policy cover?

I know I sound like a life insurance agent here, but be aware that if you don't wake up tomorrow, those close to you will be dealing with an emotional nightmare. You can't control that, but you do have the power to help them avoid a financial disaster as well.

Take some time to review your needs. If you have a spouse or part-

ner, schedule a time to talk about what would happen if one of you died. This could be one of the most important discussions of your life.

DISABILITY INSURANCE

The vision of being disabled frightens many people more than the thought of death. That's one reason why more people own life insurance than disability insurance.

During the 1960s and 1970s, the mortality rate of four major diseases (hypertension, diabetes, heart and cerebrovascular diseases) decreased dramatically. During the same period, however, the morbidity (disability) rate increased.

Single, self-employed people, and those working for small companies without disability benefits should consider buying supplementary disability insurance. If you become disabled, there may be no person or benefit program that will *adequately* replace your income during a period when your medical and personal expenses will undoubtedly increase. Without disability insurance, any well-crafted financial plan is incomplete, and your hard-earned assets are in serious jeopardy.

OTHER TYPES OF INSURANCE

A variety of other insurance products will be mentioned briefly here:
- Health insurance is critical. You should always have at least catastrophic or high-deductible coverage.
- Long-Term Care or Nursing Home coverage is something to consider as retirement approaches.
- Auto Insurance: legally and morally, you shouldn't drive a vehicle unless you have auto insurance.
- Property insurance: homeowner's or renter's coverage is needed to protect your valuable possessions and provide liability coverage for accidents on your property.
- Errors-and-omissions coverage: buy this if you are vulnerable to a lawsuit based on the work you do.
- Umbrella policies can fill in gaps in between policies.

From a financial standpoint, it is important to remain calm in the face of insurance agents and the tension that comes with making a difficult buying decision.

Early in my life insurance agent days, I heard a story about another agent. Sitting at a couple's kitchen table, he paused for emotional impact, looked at the husband, then he asked the wife, "Do you want to bury your husband like a dog?"

Your insurance needs are too important to delegate to a bully. If high-pressure tactics are being used, ask the agent to leave; there are plenty of respectable agents around. Above all, an uncomfortable situation should not be a barrier between you and the completion of your financial strategy.

WHERE THERE'S A WILL
THERE'S AN ATTORNEY

IF THERE WERE NO BAD PEOPLE, THERE WOULD BE NO GOOD LAWYERS.
CHARLES DICKENS , THE OLD CURIOSITY SHOP

To lighten things up, let's talk about wills.

I'm constantly amazed how many people don't have wills: not just people who don't have any assets, but parents with dependent children, rich folks and even attorneys. I'm not an attorney, so I cannot give legal advice. That means this chapter will be mercifully short.

Most people think wills deal only with money, but wills are especially important for parents. Though the efficient transfer of assets to heirs is important, individuals need to designate who will raise their children if both parents die prematurely. I'm going to use the word "die" here rather than "pass away;" we need to face reality, even if it makes us uncomfortable.

You may know an individual or couple whom you would like to care for your children, but you need to ask their permission and leave written instructions detailing your wishes. If you don't, a representative of your state will make that decision for you.

Do you want your weird sister-in-law Mildred raising your children? How about strange Uncle Louie? They might cherish that role since they've often told you what a poor parenting job you've done. He or she might be particularly interested in this task if it also involves unselfishly administering a substantial amount of money on your children's behalf.

There are lots of really important and uncomfortable decisions you need to make when writing a will. Though you can buy a fill-in-the-blanks will form or legal software, I advise consulting with an attorney for this task.

You've certainly heard horror stories about how once cordial family relationships became acrimonious after one or both parents die. Not only can this be an agonizing emotional experience, it can create layers of intrigue and distrust that survive within the family for decades.

It is important to develop a good working relationship with a family lawyer, someone who can advise you on a variety of legal matters or refer you to a specialist when necessary. You wouldn't wait until you are seriously ill to find a family doctor, so connect with a competent attorney before you find yourself in the midst of a stressful event.

More sophisticated estate planning strategies may be appropriate if you have a substantial estate or a complicated family situation. As one clever estate planning questionnaire asked:

If you died tomorrow, what percentage of your estate would you like to leave to the following groups? Family ____% Favorite Charities ____% Government ____%.

Revocable living trusts can be used to reduce or eliminate the cost of probate and sometimes to avoid some difficult family decisions. These popular trusts, if drawn properly, do not require that you forfeit control of your assets. Other advanced estate planning strategies can involve *irrevocable* trusts, life insurance trusts, gifting and ownership/

title changes. Consult an attorney to determine what steps are appropriate for your situation.

The prospect of your death can be quite disturbing. However, by clearly defining your last wishes, you will spare your loved ones some agonizing decisions at a time when they are already grieving. Doing these responsible things is truly an unselfish act of love.

INFORMATION OVERLOAD

AS ONE GOES THROUGH LIFE, IT IS EXTREMELY IMPORTANT TO CONSERVE FUNDS,
AND ONE SHOULD NEVER SPEND MONEY ON ANYTHING FOOLISH, LIKE PEAR
NECTAR OR A SOLID GOLD HAT.
WOODY ALLEN, WITHOUT FEATHERS

The blossoming of your financial awareness is crucial to achieving
monetary success. As you begin the investment selection process, however, don't let the vast quantity of available information emotionally
paralyze you.

If you perpetually agonize over when and what you should do with
your money, you'll miss opportunities. A mediocre decision is often
better than no decision. If you can't decide where to invest now, at least

put money into a savings account so you won't spend it before you decide.

Your reasons for hesitating may be so obscure as to be unknown even to your psychoanalyst or your hair stylist. An infinite amount of data is available from numerous resources, including financial magazines, books, radio talk shows, the Internet, and your father-in-law. Faced with so many investment options it is nearly impossible to make the perfect decision.

Don't be overly concerned with picking *the best* particular investment within the range of your risk tolerance. Try not to let this information overload keep you from making the worst mistake: becoming indecisive, or worse, returning to your old habits.

You must adopt a proper attitude about investing, otherwise you will consistently feel like a loser. Let's assume you buy a stock that doubles in price. You sell it and are rightfully proud, but then it doubles again. Don't feel like a fool: accept that you did well. No one can consistently buy stocks at their low points and sell them at their peaks.

Once you start regularly discussing stocks and mutual funds, you'll get tips from your neighbors at weekend parties. News articles about growing firms will catch your eye. Even your plumber will tout high-tech stocks while snaking out your main drain line.

> ADVICE IS WHAT WE ASK FOR WHEN WE ALREADY KNOW THE ANSWER, BUT WISH WE DIDN'T.
>
> ERICA JONG

You will agonize that you didn't have the guts and foresight to buy a thousand shares of the company that developed the cellular baby diapering machine. At some point you will notice that one of those stocks grew from $2 to $19 a share. People quickly forget about the mediocre stock tips they received, but they usually remember missed opportunities. Making financial decisions is not easy, and you are bound to make mistakes, but a bad decision is often more valuable than indecision.

One example of information overload is the mutual fund prospectus. This disclosure document is designed to help consumers make an educated decision, but sometimes the numerous disclaimers and warnings can distract investors from finding the important data:

• Minimum investment amount required to open an account,

- Sales charges,
- Annual fund expenses,
- Fund's investment policy,
- Glossy fold-out of the Portfolio Manager of the Month.

Mutual funds will soon be allowed to use plain-language fact sheets that will offer important information in a clearer form. That's a good idea because if the trend toward more disclaimers is not reversed, the prospectus of the future might look like the prospectus on the next page.

PROSPECTUS OF THE FUTURE

QESBL* Growth Mutual Fund
(*Quick Eddie's Safe But Lucrative)
Dated January 31, 2001

BEWARE: DO NOT READ ANYTHING ON THIS OR ANY FOLLOW-ING PAGE UNLESS YOU ARE WEARING SHATTER-PROOF EYEWEAR!

Do NOT eat this prospectus. The paper could clog your airways, causing a slow, painful death by suffocation.

Do NOT read this prospectus while driving a motorized vehicle. Further, you should use caution when reading this or any prospectus while riding any of the following: a skateboard, bicycle, tricycle or uni-cycle.

Because this prospectus weighs almost 28 pounds, you should use your legs, not your back when lifting it.

Do NOT turn the pages unless you are wearing protective gloves. A paper cut, if not treated immediately, could cause excessive bleeding, death or the permanent staining of an expensive business suit.

Do NOT make children read this document. Actually, only three people have read this entire document. Two are institutionalized in The Home for Deranged Contrarians in Bull Market, Idaho. The third now hosts a successful gardening show on Saturday television.

TABLE OF CONTENTS   Page

IT'S TIME TO TAKE ACTION

WHEN ASKED THE SECRET OF HIS SUCCESS, BILLIONAIRE
J. BILLIONAIRE PAUL GETTY REPLIED,
"WAKE EARLY, WORK HARD AND STRIKE OIL."

If you've read this far, you obviously have some vivid dreams and enough motivation to take control of your financial life, but be warned. There will always be reasons to delay your plans, and once you start investing, temptations to stop investing will continue to arise.

You must be tenacious in the pursuit of your dreams because a variety of barriers and distractions will impede your progress. Cars seem particularly adept at sensing when you have some extra cash available, and computers are rapidly learning this technique.

Leading a successful financial life involves knowing how you think and feel about money. If your money management is a shared activity, increased knowledge and awareness will improve communications with your spouse or partner.

Mental barriers may keep you from taking control of your financial situation. These can include:

- Fear of Success
- Fear of Failure
- Fear Of Commitment
- Fear of Financial Institutions
- Fear of Sitting on a Bulging Wallet
- Fear of Appearing Ignorant
- Guilt

A surprising number of my clients express genuine feelings of guilt about either having "too much" money or making "too much" money. If any significant mental barrier prevents you from pursuing your financial dreams, it may be in your best interest to consult a professional advisor. The Resources chapter lists some books about the psychology of money.

In the Workbook Section you can list any barriers you believe keep you from controlling your financial life. Once you can identify these obstacles, you can more easily deal with their consequences.

Some final investing tips

Don't forget that your responsibilities to your Future Self are important. Here are some suggestions to help you save or invest on a regular basis:

- Send yourself an invoice each month like your utility company does.
- Put a self-addressed envelope to your investment company in with the bills. Pay yourself first.
- Open a separate savings or mutual fund account for designated goals.
- Use automatic deductions from your paycheck or have money transferred to investments periodically from your checking account.
- Pay attention to your statements and appreciate the growth of your money.
- Make your partner aware of your progress.
- When your children are old enough, teach them how to manage their own money.

CASH. I AM JUST NOT HAPPY WHEN I DON'T HAVE IT. THE MINUTE I HAVE IT I HAVE TO SPEND IT. AND I JUST BUY STUPID THINGS.

ANDY WARHOL, FROM A TO B AND BACK AGAIN

When you become more comfortable with the process of investing, decisions and follow-through become easier. Review your progress regularly. Don't be too upset if your goals are not met over a one-year period. Likewise, don't be too gleeful if you triple those goals in a particular year. Examine your results over three year periods to see if your long-term objectives are being met.

Regularly review your goals, reassess your risk tolerance and adjust your strategy. As you continue to invest, your money garden grows while you harvest the fruits of your financial efforts.

MUCH WORK IS MERELY A
WAY TO EARN MONEY;
MUCH LEISURE IS MERELY A
WAY TO SPEND IT.
C. WRIGHT MILLS

It is OK to Spend Your Money

Throughout this book I've encouraged you to spend less and accumulate more money. These are the habits that will allow you to live your dreams, but money is ultimately for spending. By defining goals, setting deadlines and calculating the cost of your dream, you'll have a better idea when it's time to spend some of those funds you've spent years nurturing.

There is a time to plant and a time to reap. I hope you allow yourself to do both of these to your fullest potential.

VALUES-BASED INVESTING
(VBI)

SOCIAL INVESTMENT ENCOMPASSES MANY COMPLEMENTARY, THOUGH DIFFERENT,
CONCEPTS. BUT THE VARIOUS PARTS OF SOCIAL INVESTMENT SHARE A COMMON
THEME: THE INTEGRATION OF SOCIAL OR ETHICAL CRITERIA INTO THE
INVESTMENT DECISION-MAKING PROCESS.
AMY L. DOMINI, THE SOCIAL INVESTMENT ALMANAC

BUSINESS MUST ACCOUNT FOR ITS STEWARDSHIP NOT ONLY ON THE BALANCE
SHEET BUT ALSO IN MATTERS OF SOCIAL RESPONSIBILITY.
ROBERT E. WOOD, PRESIDENT OF SEARS ROEBUCK (1928-1954)

I WAS BORN WITH A MUTANT FINANCIAL GENE

(My Path to Values-Based Investing)

THE FREAN IS A SEA MONSTER WITH THE BODY OF A CRAB AND
THE HEAD OF A CERTIFIED PUBLIC ACCOUNTANT.
WOODY ALLEN, WITHOUT FEATHERS

I didn't become a "suit person" until 1979.

When I started college in 1966, I was intent on becoming a Certified Public Accountant, but I later veered from that glamorous career path. One day in my junior year, as I surveyed the other students in my Cost Accounting class, it struck me. I just didn't fit in. I was the only long-haired male in the class, and no other students were wearing jeans. I felt more comfortable in the counterculture than in the counter culture of accounting.

I realized I would probably be miserable working in a large accounting firm. I must have been born with a mutant financial gene because dealing with numbers and money came easily to me, but I just couldn't find a good way to use that skill. So I left class, walked thoughtfully to the administration building and changed my major to political science.

After graduation, I worked in political campaigns, substitute teaching positions and ran a seasonal tax preparation business. Until I answered a help-wanted ad for a "financial planner," I had not yet really started a career.

I was disturbed to learn that the job actually involved selling life insurance, but I hoped this opportunity could evolve into something more. In my prior jobs I had assisted people in a non-monetary way. With my financial acumen, I believed I could help people better manage their finances.

By 1980, I was selling mutual funds and taking classes to become a Chartered Life Underwriter (CLU) and Chartered Financial Consultant (ChFC). I looked like a Republican Congressional candidate when I discovered four or five mutual funds which would not invest in corporations that were major environmental polluters, tobacco products manufacturers, or nuclear weapons developers.

My concern for health and environmental considerations rather than just profits gradually isolated me from my professional peer group. Then I heard about the Social Investment Forum (SIF), an organization that promoted socially responsible investing (SRI) or what I now prefer to call values-based investing (VBI).

> WE MAKE A LIVING BY WHAT
> WE GET, WE MAKE A
> LIFE BY WHAT WE GIVE.
>
> *WINSTON CHURCHILL*

About 1987, I attended the SIF conference in San Francisco in search of soul mates. In the lavish foyer of the Sir Francis Drake Hotel I chatted with another attendee. He was a lot like me: a clean-cut fellow with hair just a touch longer than normal, about forty years old, and wearing a suit. As we sipped coffee from dainty porcelain cups, we discovered that we both had attended California State University at Northridge in 1970.

Our conversation immediately switched from the performance of a particular mutual fund to a pivotal day in each of our lives, the day of the big campus protest following the Kent State tragedy.

An army of L. A. police officers had surrounded our demonstration and begun to disperse the crowd. Fearing another tragedy, we each ran for our respective lives. Being careful not to drip coffee on our conservative business suits, he and I traded dramatic stories of that distressing day.

Driving home to Sacramento, I was inspired by many of the financial people I met at that meeting. I also thought of the Crosby, Stills, and Nash concert my wife and I attended the day before I left for the SIF conference. When they harmonized, "We can change the world...," it made me sad to think I had lost that belief.

But participating in the SIF Conference revived my optimism. I had met some exciting new friends who believed that we could help make the world a better place.

After that conference, I was no longer tentative about the topic, and values-based investing gradually became my specialty. Now that the number of VBI options has grown and the topic has gained greater attention, I try to ask all investment clients if they wish to avoid certain companies and industries. The vast majority, even those who don't look like they sell hemp hats for a living, tell me that they want to invest in a manner consistent with their social and environmental concerns.

DEFINING VALUES-BASED INVESTING

GOODNESS IS THE ONLY INVESTMENT THAT NEVER FAILS.
HENRY DAVID THOREAU

Even if values-based investing (VBI) is not of interest to you, I welcome you to examine a topic more commonly referred to as socially responsible investing (SRI).

As acronyms go, I prefer VBI to SRI; it just sounds less judgmental. "Responsible" implies an "I'm right and you're wrong" attitude. One person's idea of courage and social responsibility may be viewed by another as a contemptible action. Even financial advisors who specialize in this area regularly debate the issue of purity versus pragmatism while struggling to construct a working definition of this term.

The most commonly accepted VBI definition is the active avoidance or "screening out" of companies that make products or conduct business contrary to the investor's ethical beliefs. All mutual fund managers use financial criteria in their stock selection process. Values-based mutual funds managers use ethical and social criteria as well.

Some typical avoidance or negative screens that eliminate companies include:

- Cigarette, alcohol and gambling industries
- Gun and weapon system manufacturers
- Nuclear energy
- Repressive regimes and governments (formerly South Africa)
- Poor employee/customer relations or discrimination
- Firms that use foreign sweat shops and child labor

GROWTH OF ASSETS IN VALUES-BASED MUTUAL FUNDS

Year	Assets $MM	Assets % Change
1983	150	—
1984	205	37%
1985	322	57%
1986	416	29%
1987	482	16%
1988	622	29%
1989	930	50%
1990	1,146	23%
1991	1,746	52%
1992	2,346	34%
1993	2,566	9%
1994	2,399	-6%
1995	3,080	28%
1996	3,953	28%
Mar 97	4,284	8%

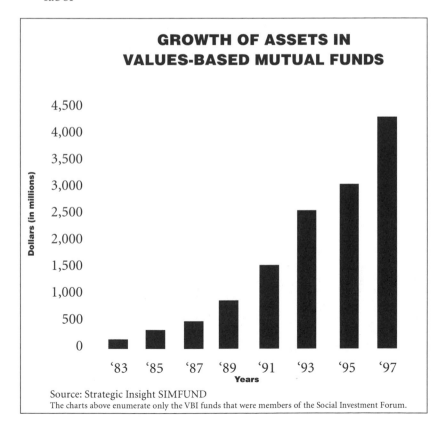

GROWTH OF ASSETS IN VALUES-BASED MUTUAL FUNDS

Source: Strategic Insight SIMFUND
The charts above enumerate only the VBI funds that were members of the Social Investment Forum.

- Unsafe or unhealthy products
- Animal cruelty or animal testing in product research
- Flagrant or chronic polluters

Many VBI mutual funds also use positive screens to select companies for investments. These attraction criteria include:

- Beneficial and safe products/services
- Superior employee/customer treatment
- Ethnic and gender diversity in top management positions and on board of directors
- Efficient use of energy & natural resources
- Community involvement/charitable giving

Specific mutual funds will not be mentioned in this book because this information gets out-

GROWTH IN NUMBER OF VALUES-BASED MUTUAL FUNDS

Year	Total Funds
1971	1
1972	2
1982	5
1983	6
1985	7
1986	8
1987	10
1990	12
1991	14
1992	25
1993	26
1994	34
1995	40
1996	43
Mar 97	47

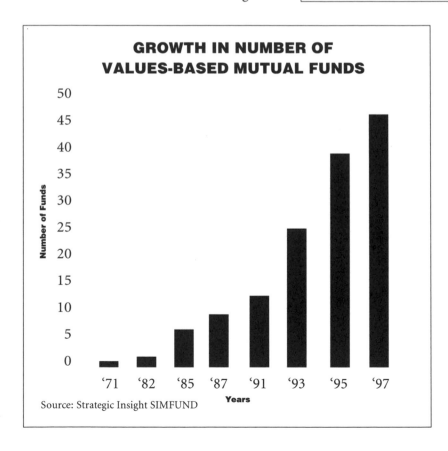

GROWTH IN NUMBER OF VALUES-BASED MUTUAL FUNDS

Source: Strategic Insight SIMFUND

dated so quickly. Please refer to the Resources chapter to access more current information on VBI funds.

Mutual funds are the most visible and easily quantifiable component of values-based investing, but public pension funds and large trusts also use social screens. According to the Social Investment Forum, $1.18 trillion is currently invested using at least one social screens. That is almost 10% of all money invested.

> HE THAT IS OF THE OPINION MONEY WILL DO EVERYTHING MAY WELL BE SUSPECTED OF DOING EVERYTHING FOR MONEY.
>
> BENJAMIN FRANKLIN

Screened mutual funds and individual stocks and bonds constitute one leg of the VBI stool; the other two "legs" are more proactive. Shareholder activism involves taking a more active role in the management of a company. The most common form is proxy voting where individual stockholders bring resolutions to a vote of all the stockholders in hopes of changing corporate policies.

> SURPLUS WEALTH IS A SACRED TRUST WHICH ITS POSSESSOR IS BOUND TO ADMINISTER IN HIS LIFETIME FOR THE GOOD OF THE COMMUNITY.
>
> ANDREW CARNEGIE

Community loan funds are the third leg, providing economic incentives and low-cost loans through progressive banks and credit unions. Some other values-based investment options include trusts designed to purchase public land for preservation purposes and social venture capital projects.

So how do you know if a mutual fund is really values based? To start with, don't depend merely on the name of the fund. Just because there's a happy-faced Earth on the prospectus' cover doesn't necessarily mean the fund is environmentally friendly. Occasionally a fund's name unfaithfully reflects the makeup of its portfolio.

Funds which use social screens will define their screening criteria in their prospectuses. Various VBI funds use different screens and apply them with different levels of intensity. A list of VBI mutual funds and money market funds can be obtained by contacting the Social Investment Forum at the address listed in the Resources chapter.

This section of Tending Your Money Garden is intended merely to introduce the topic of VBIs. To learn more, consult your local financial professional who specializes in values-based investing or read some of the books and newsletters noted in the Resources chapter.

THE DILEMMA OF
VALUES-BASED INVESTING

MAKE MONEY YOUR GOD AND IT WILL PLAGUE YOU LIKE THE DEVIL.
HENRY FIELDING

Company A was accused at a mutual fund shareholders meeting of selling a product that depletes the ozone layer.

Company B spent billions of dollars to clean up the environment in the 1990s.

Which is the socially responsible company? Of course, this is a trick question. Company B is Exxon, which spent a small fortune cleaning up Prince Edward Sound—and its corporate image—since the Valdez oil spill.

Company A is Ben and Jerry's, a firm generally perceived as being socially responsible. Their ice cream, however, requires the cooperation of cows, animals who expel bovine flatulence, a pungent gas that can deplete the ozone layer.

THE CHIEF VALUE OF MONEY LIES IN THE FACT THAT ONE LIVES IN A WORLD IN WHICH IT IS OVERESTIMATED.

H. L. MENCKEN

Here's another example. Company C is one of the highest emitters of toxic waste in the nation. Company D has one of the most innovative environmental programs in the nation and has cut toxic waste by 50% in the last five years.

Company C is Minnesota Mining and Manufacturing (3M). Company D is also 3M. Several other enormous manufacturing firms also fit both profiles.

The point I'm making here is that values-based investing is not a black and white subject. It's not a choice between Luke Skywalker and Darth Vader. Even Darth, we ultimately discovered, had some redeeming qualities, while Luke not only wore a silly haircut, but he probably had impure fantasies about Princess Leia.

On a continuum from the worst to the best company, there's an arbitrary line that separates companies you may be comfortable with from those you aren't. To complicate this process, a company that does well in one particular area may do poorly in another aspect.

Mutual fund companies that also use *social* screens hire firms such as Franklin Research & Development Corporation or Kinder, Lydenberg, Domini & Co., Inc. to do their *non-financial* research. These organizations scrutinize the policies, performance, and priorities of a wide range of corporations.

Just as there is no perfect human being, there's no such thing as the perfectly good or evil company. We all pollute and we all use natural resources in varying degrees. But we also each have the power to make the Earth a safer and healthier place for ourselves and our children.

SELL NOT VIRTUE TO PURCHASE WEALTH, NOT
LIBERTY TO PURCHASE POWER.
BENJAMIN FRANKLIN

DOMINI 400 SOCIAL INDEX℠

WITHOUT A RICH HEART WEALTH IS AN UGLY BEGGAR.
RALPH WALDO EMERSON

"How much worse are my investments going to perform if I invest consistently with my values?" I'm often asked. My unequivocal answer is, "I don't know." Stock market prognostication is not the topic of this book. How well your investments perform will depend on when and where you invest in VBIs compared to whenever and wherever you would have invested alternatively.

More generically, the question is: "Is there a cost to values-based investing?" The only quantifiable cost is the cost for the screening process, about one quarter of one per cent or less. One way to compare how screened and unscreened portfolios have performed in the past is to look at the Domini 400 Social Index.

An index is a collection of stock prices that represent a larger collection of stocks or segment of the economy. The Dow Jones Industrial Average, a collection of 30 stocks, and the broader-based Standard and Poor's 500 Stock Index are the two most famous indices.

The Domini 400 Social Index was constructed by Kinder, Lydenberg, Domini & Co., Inc., a research firm in Massachusetts which evaluates stocks based on social criteria. This index provides the most comprehensive comparison between the performance of screened and non-screened portfolios.

From the 500 stocks in the Standard and Poor's Index, KLD eliminated half of the stocks that were least in compliance with social screens they identified. Next, 100 screened stocks from underrepresented industries were added to the Domini 400 Index to rebalance its sectors relative to the S&P. Fifty others with strong social records were then selected.

Between its origin in May of 1990 and the end of 1997, the Domini Index achieved a total return of **303%**. During that same time period the S&P Index grew by **262%**. No sweeping conclusions should be drawn from this example, but it is significant to note how closely the two indexes mirror the ups and downs of the market.

COMPARISON OF THE DOMINI 400 SOCIAL INDEX FUND WITH THE STANDARD AND POOR'S 500 INDEX

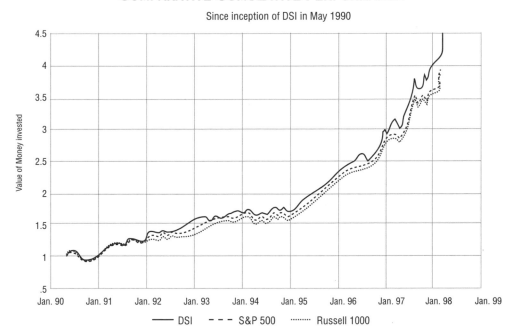

COMPARATIVE CUMULATIVE PERFORMANCE
Since inception of DSI in May 1990

Note: The performance comparison shown above is based on total return (dividends and capital gains have been reinvested).

Note: These results represent past performance and do not imply future results. Economic and market conditions change and both will cause investment return and principal value to fluctuate.

To Screen or not to Screen?

Wealth is not his that has it, but his that enjoys it.
Benjamin Franklin

I'm constantly amazed when my clients tell me about brokers or financial planners who have insulted them. These advisors attempted to make them feel foolish for caring as much about where they invested as about how much money they made.

There is a myth, and I firmly believe it is a myth, that investing with social concerns earns less money than investments without screens. Detractors point to past performance of certain VBI funds, but the majority of existing VBI funds were not available five years ago and those funds have not been tested in a "down" stock market.

My theory is that this prejudice among stock brokers against VBI's stems from their generally conservative political beliefs. VBI screens are perceived as liberal issues that taint the investment selection process. However, advocating a cleaner environment is not solely a liberal issue.

Some newer values-based funds focus on specific issues: women or ethnic-owned businesses, gay/lesbian issues and animal testing concerns. Other funds use religious or spiritual values in their stock selection process.

Critics of VBIs argue that mutual funds which limit their universe of stocks will have fewer options, so a lower rate of return may ultimately result. By considering non-financial factors, the pro-VBI response goes, you can avoid stocks that may be more prone to legal actions (i.e. tobacco companies), government fines (i.e. consistent Super Fund pollution site creators) and the long-term consequences of public relations meltdowns.

To me, companies that make a concerted effort to be good corporate citizens will ultimately be more highly valued by investors than those that care not for the consequences of their actions. I hope that some day, long-term commitments will be come more highly valued on Wall Street than short-term profits.

Each of us has a set of values and principles that guide us through life. If you believe strongly in your values, you may also wish to have your investments reflect and support those same values.

CRITICS ARGUE VALUES-BASED FUNDS WON'T PERFORM AS WELL AS VBIs BECAUSE THERE ARE FEWER STOCKS TO CHOOSE FROM

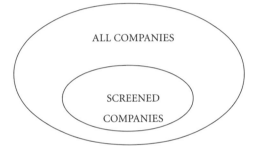

ALL COMPANIES

SCREENED COMPANIES

VBI PROPONENTS ARGUE THAT SCREENED INVESTMENTS WILL PERFORM AS WELL AS UNSCREENED FUNDS BECAUSE THEY ARE LESS LIKELY TO FACE THE FOLLOWING RISKS WHICH WILL HAVE LONG-TERM NEGATIVE FINANCIAL IMPACTS ON THE PRICE OF A STOCK:

• EPA AND GOVERNMENT AGENCY FINES
• PRODUCT LIABILITY LEGAL ACTIONS
• BAD PUBLIC RELATIONS
• DECLINE IN SALES OF UNHEALTHY/POOR PRODUCTS

ALWAYS DO RIGHT. THIS WILL GRATIFY SOME
PEOPLE, AND ASTONISH THE REST.
MARK TWAIN

EPILOGUE

Hiking Half Dome

Hiking Half Dome

LIVE YOUR LIFE EACH DAY AS YOU WOULD CLIMB A MOUNTAIN. AN OCCASIONAL
GLANCE TOWARDS THE SUMMIT KEEPS THE GOAL IN MIND, BUT MANY BEAUTIFUL
SCENES ARE TO BE OBSERVED FROM EACH NEW VANTAGE POINT.
HAROLD B. MELCHART

Why, you ask, is a chapter about hiking to the top of Yosemite's majestic Half Dome included in a book about managing your money? Mainly because I've got three trays of slides you must see some day. But seriously, undertaking a challenging hike has much in common with pursuing a financial goal.

So, please accompany me on this mini-adventure as I reiterate some of the key components of successful money management that I've mentioned throughout this book.

!Beware of Falling Analogies and Slippery Similes!

The flat face of Half Dome looks down on Yosemite Valley, a sentinel admiring the beauty below. This massive rock has always fascinated me, yet until my wife, son and I hiked to the top in 1996, I had never thought I'd be standing up there experiencing that splendid view.

That August day was one of the more arduous and harrowing days of my life. Despite spending weeks of preparation getting into shape, I still worried that the climb would be too physically exhausting. Also, not being one to seek out bodily risk, dealing with my fear was as much a challenge as the physical exertion. This eight mile hike became a quest—-something I needed to do.

As I dragged myself along dusty trails and up giant rock staircases, I began to compare this trek with the process of trying to achieve lofty financial goals. Since my brain is cursed with a mechanism that constantly thinks in terms of analogies, I began to list **the steps common**

to physical and fiscal challenges.

Start early. Rising at 4:30, we dressed, stretched, packed and set out on the trail guided by our flashlights. As we approached the trailhead, our goal, the distinctive Half Dome, rose as an awesome silhouette a mile above Yosemite Valley. Reaching the top looked like an impossible feat from that vantage point, but we knew that hundreds of people complete that climb every summer day.

As with most daunting tasks, we had to **focus on intermediate goals:** climbing the Vernal Falls mist trail, following the steps to the top of Nevada Falls, hiking the long stretch through the forest of Little Yosemite Valley, then proceeding up the steady incline where we passed above the tree line.

One thousand stone stairs lead to the base of the sheer "back" side of Half Dome. The more steps we climbed, the harder the task became, yet **we stuck to our goal.**

The final challenge to Half Dome's broad summit is a 45 to 70 degree grade. Hikers use handholds made of two steel cables four feet apart. About every fifteen feet along this cable pathway, posts are sunk into the granite. Two-by-four boards cross this path, allowing hikers a chance to rest.

Stacey led, followed by our son Ross, who was then thirteen. One-third of the way up the cables he started to panic. Stacey's supportive words calmed him, and we continued moving upward on the nearly vertically path. I followed just behind him, my role switching between that of protective father and that of solitary hiker grasping the cables as if my life depended on them (which it did).

Soon, the closeness of the goal neutralized my sense of danger and our collective weariness. When the cables ended and the incline flattened into the enormous surface of Half Dome, we knew we had reached our goal. **Having worked hard and overcome our fears, we celebrated** with a family hug.

The hour we spent on top of Half Dome was glorious. We viewed Yosemite Valley below, Nature's Disneyland, and admired the panorama of the mighty Sierra Nevada peaks that surrounded us.

I scooched slowly toward the edge, finally hanging my legs over the ledge. I looked down at the Valley, five thousand feet directly below.

This moment was what I had envisioned every time I'd dreamed of this hike.

We ate lunch sitting on the warm granite, sharing this spectacular setting with about one hundred others who had made the climb. We did our best to ignore the marmots who begged us to share our food.

Too soon, it was time to put our gloves back on and start back down the cables. Though not nearly as exhausting as pulling ourselves up the mountain, the descent was much more frightening. When we planned this hike **we knew what the barriers and risks might be. That did not eliminate our fears but the reward justified the risk.** We shared the cables with apprehensive climbers descending below us and squeezed past exhausted ones climbing upward.

I'm not usually afraid of heights, but this was an experience of a different magnitude. I had to focus on the next two-by-four rather than looking at ant-sized hikers far below. When a task is difficult, it **is sometimes necessary to focus on very short-term goals.**

After four hours of constant hiking, the most dangerous portion was behind us. **I looked back and appreciated the progress we had made.** To me, going down seems as if it should be easier, but steep downgrades and stairs can be punishing, particularly when you are already exhausted.

We reached the trailhead at five in the afternoon, twelve hours after we had begun. Nearly every muscle in my 47-year old body ached. I felt twice my age, but was proud that we had achieved our goal and created a vivid family memory that will forever stay with us.

It was time to rest and reflect on the lessons of the day. **When striving toward a lofty dream, accept that there will be risks and obstacles,** whether they may be a twisted ankle or the financial equivalent of a coiled rattlesnake blocking your path. However, **once you reach your goal it is important to reward yourself.** We indulged ourselves with a lavish dinner at the Ahwahnee Hotel.

That night, I reflected that life's journey doesn't come with a topographical map, and while planning and preparation are crucial, you can never be certain what lies ahead. So keep moving forward toward your goals, but remember to stop often to admire the view and appreciate where you are right now.

WORKBOOK
SECTION

HE WHO WOULD MAKE SERIOUS USE OF HIS LIFE
MUST ALWAYS ACT AS THOUGH HE HAD A LONG
TIME TO LIVE AND MUST SCHEDULE HIS TIME AS
IF HE WERE ABOUT TO DIE.
ÉMILE LITTRÉ

WORKBOOK SECTION

The following forms and questions can be used to help you commit yourself to more efficient money management.

You may wish to make copies of these pages first. If more than one of you handles money matters, you should each fill out these forms, then review them together. Also you may choose to update your concerns and progress at a future date.

Today's Date_____ Name: _____

DESCRIBE YOUR DREAMS

Be as specific as you can when describing your dreams. Estimate how much these financial goals will cost and set a date for completion. You might want to write a separate essay describing your dreams in more detail.

SHORT-TERM DREAM (within 2 Years)
Projected Completion Date: _____
Estimated Amount You Need to Accumulate $ _____
Describe Your Dream:_____

_____

_____

_____

INTERMEDIATE-TERM DREAM (within 7 Years)

Projected Completion Date: _____

Estimated Amount You Need to Accumulate $ _____

Describe Your Dream: _____

_____

_____

_____

LONG-TERM DREAM

Projected Completion Date: _____

Estimated Amount You Need to Accumulate $ _____

Describe Your Dream: _____

_____

_____

_____

RETIREMENT

Your Projected Retirement Age: _____

Describe what your retirement will be like: _____

_____

_____

_____

_____

_____

_____

_____

_____

_____

Today's Date_____ Name: _____

BALANCE SHEET

ASSETS		LIABILITIES	
Personal Residence (estimated value)	$ _____	First Mortgage	$ _____
		Second Mortgage _____	$
Other Real Estate	$ _____	Mortgage	$ _____
Automobile	$ _____	Auto Loan	$ _____
Automobile	$ _____	Auto Loan	$ _____
Investment Assets (list separately)		**Medium Term Debts**	
Retirement Plans	$ _____	Line of Credit	$ _____
IRAs	$ _____		
Mutual Funds	$ _____		
Stocks	$ _____		
Liquid Assets		**Short-Term Debt**	
Certificates of Deposit	$ _____	Credit Cards (list below)	$ _____
Savings Accounts	$ _____		
Checking Account	$ _____	Personal Loans	$ _____
TOTAL ASSETS	$ _____	TOTAL LIABILITIES	$ _____

NET WORTH (ASSETS-LIABILITIES) = $ _____

Credit Card Summary

Name of Card	Account Number	Current Balance	Monthly Payment	Interest Rate	Date to be Paid Off
_____	_____	$_____	$_____	____%	_____
_____	_____	$_____	$_____	____%	_____
_____	_____	$_____	$_____	____%	_____
TOTAL		$_____	$_____		

Today's Date_____ Name: _____

EVALUATE YOUR FINANCIAL RISK/REWARD EXPECTATIONS
(CHAPTER 14)

In noting your expectations, you can use a specific percentage, a percentage above the inflation rate or the return from a particular index or benchmark, such as the S&P 500.

What is the **MINIMUM** average annual return you would hope to achieve during the next five years (be realistic now):

_____%

_____% above the inflation rate

_____% above/below the _____ Index

Over a time period of a minimum of 5 years, what is the **ANTICI-PATED** average annual return you would hope to achieve:

_____%

_____% above the inflation rate

_____% above/below the _____ Index

Over time, the value of your investments will fluctuate up AND down. During one calendar year, what percentage **DECREASE** in your account value would make you so uncomfortable that it would not be worth the benefits of a higher long-term return? _____%

What do you anticipate will be the average rate of inflation over the next 5 years? _____% (see inflation chapter for history)

Investment Risk Tolerance Appraisal:
Note your current risk tolerance level by initialing on triangle below:

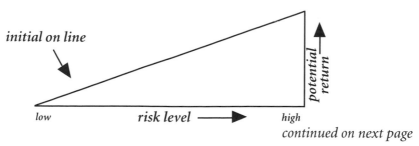

initial on line

potential return

low   *risk level* ⟶   high

continued on next page

Concerning your investments, rank the following from 1 (most) to 5 (least) in terms of how your assets are now distributed and how you would like to have them allocated a year from now.

	In One
Now	Year
___Preserve investment value with low price fluctuation.	_____
___Generate high current income with low to moderate risk.	_____
___Achieve investment growth with moderate current income.	_____
___Achieve strong investment growth with minimal income.	_____
___Maximum investment growth with no current income needs.	_____

Today's Date_____ Name: _____

INVESTMENT OBJECTIVES AND PRIORITIES

The following questions should help you prioritize your objectives:
Rank each specific financial task by degree of importance:
(10 = Crucial, need to start working on that goal next weekend.
1 = Unnecessary)

Develop and use an effective budget _____

Eliminate consumer debt _____

Create an investment program _____

Transfer funds to values-based investments _____

Establish insurance plans: health _____

                                life _____

                                disability _____

Preserve current assets _____

Buy a home _____

Pay off home mortgage early _____

Provide funds for child/children _____

Meet retirement income needs _____

Build cash fund for emergencies _____

Write or revise will or see an
attorney to update estate plan. _____

Other   1. _____   _____

         2. _____   _____

         3. _____   _____

Today's Date_____ Name: _____

WHAT IS HOLDING YOU BACK?

List the barriers that are blocking you from becoming more financially successful:

Barrier: _____

What you can do to reduce this barrier: _____

_____

Date to reevaluate: _____

_____

Barrier: _____

What you can do to reduce this barrier: _____

_____

_____

Date to reevaluate: _____

Today's Date_____ Name: _____

IT'S TIME TO TAKE ACTION

First, review your dreams and your priorities.
Now, list three actions you will take within one week to help you achieve more control of your financial situation.

1. _____
   _____

2. _____
   _____

3. _____
   _____

Date one week from today: _____

INITIAL INVESTMENT PLAN
(for first time investors)

Initial amount of money you plan to invest within 3 months $_____
Do you plan to add money on a regular basis or at any time during the next 2 years? _____
Describe what this money is ultimately to be used for: _____
_____

When is the soonest you feel you will need the money you plan to invest (assuming there will be no significant unforeseen circumstances)?
_____years

Can it be used for *any* other purposes?_____
_____

Today's Date_____ Name: _____

VALUES-BASED INVESTING PREFERENCES

If you wish to use non-financial criteria to select your investments, I've noted some common areas of concern. If it is important for you to invest in line with your values, the following list may help. Blank spaces are available if you have preferences different from these.

Do you wish to consider non-financial factors concerning any of the following industries?

___Tobacco manufacturer

___Alcohol producers

___Gambling industries

___Gun and weapon system manufacturers

___Nuclear energy generators and component manufacturers

___US Government Treasury Bills

___ _____

Do you wish to consider non-financial factors concerning companies with any of the following characteristics?

___Flagrant polluters /Chronic EPA regulations violators

___Do substantial business with repressive regimes and governments

___Have poor employee/customer relations or history of discrimination

___Use foreign sweat shops and child labor

___History of manufacturing unsafe or unhealthy products

___History of animal cruelty during product tests

___Use any form of animal testing

___ _____

Would you like to invest in companies with the following characteristics?

___Beneficial and safe products/services

___Superior employee/customer treatment

___Ethnic and gender diversity in top management positions and on board of directors

___Efficient or alternative use of energy & natural resources

___Tolerant policies toward alternative lifestyles

___Community involvement/charitable giving

___ _____

Resources

RESOURCES
(selected reading and Websites)

General financial planning, investment advice and money management books abound. This section will only mention books and websites for selected categories. If you have an interest in either of these areas, I hope this helps you explore the topic further.

GENERAL MONEY TOPICS/ MENTAL ASPECTS OF MONEY
Money and the Meaning of Life by Jacob Needleman. Doubleday/Currency Books, New York, NY. 1991.

The New Century Family Money Book by Jonathan Pond. Dell Publishing. 1995.

The Oxford Book of Money edited by Kevin Jackson, Oxford University Press, Oxford. A collection of essays, poems and quotes about various aspects of money. 1995.

Think and Grow Rich by Napoleon Hill. Fawcett Crest Books, New York, NY. 1960. Motivational.

The Truth about Living Trusts by Nan Goodart, Dearborn Financial Publishing, Inc. Chicago, Il 60606. 1995.

You and Money: Would it be all right with you if life got easier? by Maria Nemeth, Ph.D. Vildehiya Publications, 1281 47th Ave., Sacramento, CA 95831. 1997.

Your Money or Your Life by Joe Dominguez and Vicki Robin. Penguin Books, New York, NY. 1992.

Your Money Personality: What It Is and How You Can Profit from It by Kathleen Gurney, Ph.D. Doubleday, New York, NY. 1988.

VALUES-BASED INVESTING

Beyond the Bottom Line: How America's Top Corporations are Proving that Sound Business Ethics Means Good Business by Tad Tuleja. A Penguin Book, New York, NY. 1985

Investing for Good: Making Money While Being Socially Responsible by Peter Kinder, Steven Lydenberg and Amy Domini. Harper Business, New York, NY. 1993

Investing From the Heart: The Guide to Socially Responsible Investments and Money Management by Jack Brill and Alan Reder. Crown Publishers, Inc., New York, NY. 1992

Natural Investing by Jack Brill, Hal Brill and Cliff Feigenbaum. Due out in spring of 1999. naturalinvesting.com

The Social Investment Almanac: A Comprehensive Guide to Socially Responsible Investing by Peter Kinder, Steven Lydenberg and Amy Domini. Henry Holt, New York, NY. 1992

ORGANIZATIONS/WEBPAGES
Note: all addresses are preceded by "http://www."

Calvert Group - Know What You Own Site (Shows tobacco company holdings of many mutual funds) *calverrtgoup.com/kwyo/index.html*

Co-op America *coopamerica.org*

First Affirmative Financial Network *firstaffirmative.com*

Green Money Journal *greenmoney.com*

International Association for Financial Planning *iafp.org*

Investment Company Institute: Mutual Fund Connections *ici.org*

Kinder, Lydenberg, Domini & Co., Inc. *kld.com*

Social Investment Forum *socialinvest.org*

Good Money *goodmoney.com*

GLOSSARY

MONEY, NOUN: A
BLESSING THAT IS OF NO
ADVANTAGE TO US EXCEPT
WHEN WE PART WITH IT.
*AMBROSE PIERCE, THE
DEVIL'S DICTIONARY*

Glossary

- **aardwolf:** a kind of hyena inhabiting southern Africa.

- **annuity:** a financial product that defers taxation of earnings until money is withdrawn. It can provide a series of payments based on life expectancy.

- **asset:** anything one owns that another would buy; something one owns that has commercial or exchange value.

- **balance sheet:** a statement of financial position at a given time. Lists assets and liabilities.

- **balanced:** composed of stocks and bonds, as in balanced mutual fund or balanced portfolio.

- **basis:** the amount for which an asset was purchased plus any additions to basis (such as improvements to rental property or taxable dividends to mutual funds).

- **benchmark:** an index or composite of certain stocks used for comparison purposes.

- **bear:** someone who believes that the stock market will decline. See Bull.

- **bear market:** a long period when the stock market is generally going down in value.

- **beneficiary:** the recipient of funds or property from a life insurance policy, will, or estate.

- **bond:** 1) an IOU or promissory note of a corporation or governmental body. Contains a written promise by a borrower to repay a fixed amount on a specified date and, usually, in the meantime to pay a set annual rate of interest at periodic intervals. 2) James, Agent 007.

- **bull:** 1) a person who believes that the stock market will rise. 2) description of advice from a financial advisor who guarantees you will make 30% on your money every year.

- **bull market:** a period when the stock market is going up.

- **caliphygian:** having shapely buttocks (really, it's in the dictionary).

- **capital gain or capital loss:** profit or loss from the sale of a capital asset. A short-term capital gain is taxed at the reporting individual's full income tax rate. A long-term capital gain is taxed at a lower tax rate.

- **cash flow:** the amount of cash generated over time from an investment, usually after any tax effects. Also used in personal or business situations to describe the ability to spend money from current income without going into debt.

- **CFP:** Certified Financial Planner.

- **ChFC:** Chartered Financial Consultant.

- **CLU:** Chartered Life Underwriter.

- **community development investment:** grant, loan or equity investment made primarily to support or encourage community development.

- **community property:** form of ownership between married couples available in "community property states." At the death of one spouse, entire property is passed to surviving spouse.

- **contrarian:** type of investor who selects out-of-favor stocks or invests contrary to the majority of investors.

- **corporation:** a form of business ownership. It is a separate legal unit organized under state laws which has a continuous life span independent from its ownership.

- **CPA:** Certified Public Accountant.

- **debt:** what is owed. In terms of securities, corporate borrowing using bonds, debentures, or commercial paper.

- **disclaimer:** statement or warning that clarifies liabilities or limits responsibilities.

- **diversification:** the spreading of risk between various types of assets.

- **Dow Jones Index:** an index of 30 stocks used to summarize how the bigger company stocks performed in the stock market.

- **dividend:** a payment made from earnings to the stockholders of a corporation or mutual fund.

- **dividend yield:** the ratio of the current dividend to the current price of a share of stock.

- **dollar cost averaging:** a system of buying securities at regular intervals for various prices using the same investment amount.

- **EA:** Enrolled Agent.

- **empowermint:** lozenge taken by Super Heroes to freshen their breath.

- **equity:** ownership.

- **ethics:** standards of conduct or moral judgment.

- **explication:** explanation.

- **family of mutual funds:** group of funds administered by the same company. Generally, transfers between funds within a family avoid new sales charges, but may be considered a sale for tax purposes.

- **gift:** property or property rights or interest freely transferred for less than an adequate and full consideration to another, whether the transfer is in trust or direct.

- **government bonds:** obligations of the U.S. Government. These are regarded as the highest grade of debt securities in existence.

- **grantor:** person who creates a trust.

- **groat:** a 17th century British coin.

- **index:** (1) a means of measuring the performance of a financial market through the combined prices of some or all of that market's constituents. (2) To manage assets with the objective of approximating the performance of an index.

- **interest:** payment a borrower pays a lender for the use of money.

- **investment:** the use of money for the purpose of making more money in order to gain income, increase capital, or both.

- **IRA:** individual retirement account, a type of tax-favored individual retirement plan.

- **irrevocable trust:** trust where the grantor gives up significant control of the asset, though he or she could still receive income from it. The trust is a separate tax-paying entity.

- **joint tenancy with rights of survivorship (JTWRS):** the holding of property by two or more persons in such a manner that, upon the death of one, the survivor or survivors take the entire property.

- **liability:** a debt or legal obligation to pay, shown on the right side of a balance sheet.

- **liquid assets:** 1) cash or assets that can readily be converted into cash. 2) something a winery lists on the left side of a balance sheet.

- **load:** the portion of the offering price of shares of a mutual fund which covers sales commissions and all other costs of distribution.

- **marmot:** large rodent related to the squirrel.

- **money market fund:** a type of mutual fund which invests in short-term government securities, commercial paper, and repurchase agreements.

- **mortgage:** a debt placed on real property. The debtor gives this to the creditor to secure the obligation.

- **municipal bond:** a bond issued by a state or a political subdivision, such as a county, city, town or village. In general, the interest paid on municipal bonds is exempt from federal income taxes and state and local income taxes within the state of issue.

- **mutual fund**: an investment company that collects money from investors to invest in the securities of other companies. Money invested is managed by investment advisors for the benefit of all shareholders. Mutual funds are traded securities.

- **naughty**: wayward, not behaving well.

- **net worth**: an amount reached by subtracting the value of all liabilities from the value of all assets.

- **no-load fund**: a mutual fund on which no sales commission is paid.

- **OINTMENT**: Organization for Intentionally Non-Traditional but Mostly Erroneous and Notorious Turgidity, a fictitious organization.

- **options**: aggressive investment strategy used for short-term trading.

- **over the counter**: unlisted securities not traded on a major exchange.

- **paradigms**: 20 cents.

- **pecuniary**: relating to, or consisting of money.

- **principal**: the amount originally invested. Does not include earnings.

- **prospectus**: a document which describes a mutual fund or new security line.

- **prudent**: exercising forethought.

- **revocable trust**: a trust that can be changed or terminated during the grantor's lifetime and the property recovered. Income is taxed to the grantor.

- **rhombus**: equilateral but not right-angled parallelogram or diamond.

- **risk tolerance**: your emotional comfort level with investment risk. The higher your risk tolerance, the more comfortable you are with riskier investments.

- **Roth IRA**: a kind of IRA created in 1997. Contributions do not reduce current income tax, but when funds are properly withdrawn, no tax is due.

- **security**: a financial instrument that is commonly traded on securities exchanges or markets.

- **selling short**: selling a security you don't actually own. You profit if the price declines over a short term.

- **SEP**: simplified employee pension plans. A type of IRA for self-employed individuals and certain organizations.

- **simile**: a figure of speech in which two unlike things are compared.

- **social investment**: an investment that combines an investor's financial objectives with his or her commitment to social concerns, such as peace, social justice, economic development, or a healthy environment.

- **social screen**: a non-financial criterion or set of criteria applied in the investment decision-making process. Screens can be negative (avoidance) screens or positive (attraction) screens.

- **Standard and Poor's 500 Index**: an index representing performance of large company stocks. It is used as a benchmark to summarize the performance of the stock market.

- **stock**: securities which represent an ownership interest in a corporation.

- **tangible assets**: "hard" assets such as gold, silver and collectibles.

- **tenants in common**: the holding of property by two or more persons in such a manner that, upon the death of one, the deceased's share goes to someone other than the joint tenant.

- **term insurance**: a type of life insurance that is bought for a certain period of time. Rates increase periodically. Initially, it is the cheapest type of life insurance.

- **Treasury Bill or T Bill**: a short-term bond issue by the U.S. Treasury. Considered one of the safest investments.

- **umbrella insurance policy:** an insurance policy designed to cover losses in excess of the limits of other liability policies or to cover events not covered by the other policies.

- **universal life:** a flexible type of life insurance that has an investment or interest component.

- **uvula:** pendent fleshy part of the soft palate.

- **willies:** creepy feeling, as in "gives me the willies."

- **whole life insurance:** a type of life insurance that pays a benefit if the insured dies but also has a "savings" feature that accumulates value over the life of the policy.

- **yield:** also known as return. The dividends or interest paid by a company expressed as a percentage of the current price.

- **zephyr:** gentle breeze, a west wind, or Bob's car.

ABOUT BOB DREIZLER

Bob was born in New Kensington, Pennsylvania on August 18th, 1948. He grew up in Redondo Beach, California. After graduating in Political Science from CSU, Northridge, Bob obtained a high school teaching credential with a minor in Economics. In 1980 he received a Master's Degree in Government from CSU, Sacramento.

Except for two extended travel adventures, Bob and his wife Stacey have lived in Sacramento since 1972. They have two children, Sonya and Ross.

Bob started his income tax preparation and tax planning business in 1975. Three years later he added life, disability and health insurance to the products he provides for his clients. The next year, he obtained his license to sell mutual funds and variable annuities. Bob earned his Chartered Life Underwriter (CLU) designation in 1983 and became a Chartered Financial Consultant (ChFC) in 1985.

Bob specializes in helping socially concerned individuals, families and organizations work to meet their financial goals.

He served as president of the Sacramento chapter of the International Association for Financial Planning from 1997-1998.

Between 1995 and 1997, Bob's commentaries appeared regularly in the *Sacramento Bee's* "Minding Your Money" column. From 1988 until 1992, he wrote an alternative financial column for the *Suttertown News*.

Bob's financial, humorous and personal essays have appeared in more than a dozen publications including *The San Francisco Examiner, Financial Planning, Comic Press News, Outdoor Family, Sacramento News and Review, Laf!, Sacramento Business Journal* and *Comstock's Magazine*.

ORDER FORM

Just in case you want to give a friend a copy of Tending Your Money Garden

Telephone Orders:
Call Toll Free: 1 (800) 929-7889.
Have your, VISA or MasterCard ready.

Postal Orders:
Enclose your check made out to: "Rossonya Books"
Mail to: 3104 O Street, Suite # 324,
Sacramento, CA 95816

Please send _____ copies $14.95 each. $ _____
Sales tax: Please add 7.75%
for books shipped to California addresses. $ _____
Shipping: $3.75 for the first book
and $2.00 for each additional book. $ _____
TOTAL $ _____

Name: _____

Address: _____

City _____

State _____Zip:_____ - _____

Telephone (_____) _____

Mail in your order or
call toll free and order now